With MERCY *and with* JUDGMENT

Dr. Alexander Whyte (1836-1921)

With MERCY *and with* JUDGMENT

BY

ALEXANDER WHYTE, D.D.

WITH MERCY AND WITH JUDGMENT
MY WEB OF TIME HE WOVE.

Complete and Unabridged

Shoals, Indiana

With Mercy and With Judgment

PUBLISHED BY KINGSLEY PRESS
PO Box 973
Shoals, IN 47581
USA

Tel. (800) 971-7985
www.kingsleypress.com
E-mail: sales@kingsleypress.com

ISBN: 978-1-937428-32-7 (paperbook)
ISBN: 978-1-937428-50-1 (ebook)

First Kingsley Press edition 2013

Contents

Publisher's Foreword 7
Preface 9

Part One
O the Depth of the Riches

1. The Omnipresence of God 13
2. The Image of God 21
3. The Strappado 33
4. Look to Your Motives 39
5. The Individual and His Salvation 47
6. The Element of Time in Our Devotions 55
7. A Wonder in Heaven 61

Part Two
Mercy and Truth Are Met Together

8. The Locust-Eaten Past 71
9. What Think Ye of Christ? 79
10. The Corn of Wheat 87
11. The Master and His Friends 97
12. The Honourable Name 105
13. A Great Gospel Text 113
14. The Four Winds 121

Part Three
In Remembrance of Me

15. The Comforts of God 131
16. The Evangelical Prophet 139
17. The Ransom 147

18. Crucified with Christ 155
19. To the Uttermost.. 163
20. The New Wine of the Kingdom 169

Part Four
Last Messages

21. A Study in the Swelling of Jordan... 177
22. The Hebrew Child's Question at the Passover Supper 185

Publisher's Foreword

In January of 2012, Kingsley Press published a volume of sermons on prayer by Dr. Alexander Whyte called *Lord, Teach Us to Pray*. At that time I wrote a publisher's foreword, most of which would equally apply to this book, so if you've already read that foreword, please forgive the repetition in some of what follows.

One of the enduring memories of my visits to the home of Patricia St. John, author of such timeless children's classics as *Treasures of the Snow* and *The Tanglewood's Secret*, is her profound appreciation for two books of sermons by Dr. Alexander Whyte: *Lord, Teach us to Pray* and *With Mercy and With Judgment*. I have no recollection of her ever talking to me about other books, but for these she seemed to have a deep respect—I almost said reverence.

Perhaps this appreciation for Dr. Whyte's writings had been passed down to her from her father, who, when asked which commentaries he would recommend as helps to Bible study, replied: "A man who deals with Scripture has a conscience which needs to be trained, a heart which must be warmed, and a will that should be yielded, and, finally, a mind which must be fed. For the conscience, none is better than Alexander Whyte—his *Lord, Teach Us to Pray* and *With Mercy and With Judgment* will make his readers hot and ashamed." [For the rest of his answer, see chapter 11, "The Bible Student" in his biography, *Harold St. John: A Portrait by His Daughter*, available from Kingsley Press.]

Dr. Alexander Whyte (1836–1921) was widely acknowledged to be the greatest Scottish preacher of his day, and his influence was deep and far-reaching. David McCasland, in his amazing biography of Oswald Chambers, notes that as a student, Chambers was influenced by Whyte at a deep level. Whyte was a great pulpit orator, but he was also a dedicated teacher. After preaching the Sunday evening service, he would come down from the pulpit and teach a class of about 500 young men, informally but with great intensity, for about 45 minutes. Just before dismissing them, he would state three or four questions for them to consider during their reading that week. The first year Chambers attended, Whyte conducted a series on "The Mystics," where he discussed the spiritual lives and writings of people like Tauler, Thomas à Kempis, Luther, Teresa, St. John of the Cross, Madame Guyon and Fenelon. Another year, he did a series on "The Great Autobiographies." He loved great books and would recommend them to his listeners. McCasland writes, "Many times Chambers saw him hold aloft a battered old volume with loving care as he urged his audience, 'Sell your beds and buy it.'"

Warren Wiersbe has written a short biographical sketch of Whyte in his *50 People Every Christian Should Know*. He emphasizes Whyte's diligence and hard work in sermon preparation, his warm pastoral heart, and his "surgical" preaching. He especially recommends the biography of Whyte written by G. F. Barbour.

As with *Lord, Teach Us to Pray,* editing of the text has been limited to the removing of (what we now consider) superfluous commas, and once in a great while the splitting of a very long sentence by the insertion of a period. British spelling and usage has been retained throughout.

Edward Cook
Kingsley Press
June, 2013

Preface

The welcome given to the volume of Dr. Whyte's sermons on prayer, *Lord, Teach Us to Pray,* has encouraged the hope that a more general volume might also be acceptable. That hope has been turned into a certainty by many specific requests, and the present volume is the result.

Dr. Whyte has left so much behind him of weight, worth and beauty that it has been difficult to find a principle of selection. It was desired to make this volume representative of all periods of his ministry, but much of what he used in earlier years was recast by himself, both for pulpit use and for publication in the *Bible Characters* and other books. The later sermons were also found to be on the whole more readable than the earlier. Again and again, in comparing the earlier and the later forms of one sermon, it was found that the later had gained in conciseness and force. The oldest sermon in this volume, that on "The Image of God in Man," dates from 1882. It is also the longest, and in its massive, logical style, it may be felt to bring with it the atmosphere of the earlier period when Dr. Whyte's preaching was more closely reasoned and less imaginative than it afterwards became.

It was obvious that this volume must include some of the Communion messages, which abide among the most precious spiritual memories of the people of St. George's. There is included among those given here the sermon on the Ransom, which, on the testimony of many witnesses, was an unforgettable event in the spiritual life of those who heard it. Sir William Robertson Nicoll, who was present that morning, wrote at the time of the "rare wealth of imagination and emotion" which was poured into that discourse. Scarcely less moving is the prolonged soliloquy of the sermon, "I Am Crucified with Christ," or the imaginative power of that on "The New Wine of the Kingdom." A special historical interest also attaches itself to two final messages of his long ministry—that on "The Swelling of Jordan," which was the last he was able to preach, and that on "The Hebrew Child's Question," which was prepared for a Communion service, but which he was unable to deliver.

The first section of this volume, containing sermons of a more general type, has fallen of its own accord into two parts, though no absolute division is possible. One of the wonders of Dr. Whyte's ministry was its enlarging and deepening power. Sometimes the deepening was intellectual. Sometimes again it was the imagination or the conscience that was stimulated; or his hearers suddenly felt their devotional life to be far smaller and poorer than it might have been. The first few sermons will be found to be more or less of this type. The second group has scarcely less of this quality, though on the whole it comes closer still to the evangelistic side of Dr. Whyte's message. In general theme this group and the Communion section might have been blended together.

The title for the whole volume has been chosen from the hymn which was most closely associated with Dr. Whyte's ministry and which he chose perhaps oftener than any other for the close of a service. No sermon he ever preached was far from the twofold theme of mercy and judgment; and the sea of glass mingled with fire is no unfitting symbol of the eternal realities as he saw them and proclaimed them.

J. M. E. Ross

PART ONE
O the Depth of the Riches

1

The Omnipresence of God

Whither shall I flee from Thy presence? (Psa. 139:7)
Do not I fill heaven and earth? saith the Lord (Jer. 23:24).
Lo, I am with you alway, even unto the
end of the world. Amen (Matt. 28:20).

My discourse this morning will be *De Natura Deorum*—that is to say, concerning the Divine Nature.

But to begin with, let us look for one moment at the actual word "nature" simply by itself. "All flesh is not the same flesh," says the apostle in one of his high arguments. "But there is one kind of flesh of men, another flesh of beasts, another of fishes, and another of birds." Now by his word "flesh" in that passage, the apostle means the same thing, exactly, that we mean when we employ our well-known word "nature." It is exactly as if he had said—"All nature is not the same nature. But there is one nature of men, another nature of beasts, another of fishes, and another of birds." In our classification of created things we speak first of the "nature" of earths and minerals. Ascending to the kingdom of created things immediately above the earths and minerals, we come to the "nature" of grasses and plants and trees and all things of that kind. And then we rise to the "nature" of animals. Above the nature of mere animals, again, we rise to our own "human nature," in its "four-fold state" of man unfallen; man fallen, and sinful, and mortal; man redeemed, and renewed, and restored; and man perfectly sanctified and for ever glorified. While, rising a little higher than man, we come next to the "nature" of the angels.

And then, at an absolutely infinite exaltation, we ascend to the "Divine Nature."

Now, if you were to go back upon all that, and were to ask of me just what is an earth or a mineral, I would answer your inquiry by telling you some of the attributes and characteristic qualities that, all taken together, make an earth what it is. And in the same way I would describe to you a plant, and in like manner an animal. And in like manner, a man. I would say to you that "God created man after His own image, in knowledge, righteousness, and holiness." And then, if you asked me to go on to define to you the "nature" of angels, I would say to you that I could not do it. I could only tell you that "they are all ministering spirits, sent forth to minister to them who shall be heirs of salvation." And if you still went on to interrogate me as to the "Divine Nature;" if you put this question to me, "What is God?" I would be content to answer you in the words which I have myself been taught: "God is a spirit, infinite, eternal, and unchangeable, in His being, wisdom, power, holiness, justice, goodness, and truth."

Now the omnipresence of God is that glorious attribute of the Divine Nature on which we are to meditate this morning. And it will demand all our powers of meditation. God's omnipresence—that is to say, God's presence everywhere and wholly everywhere. God's presence with all His creatures of all kinds and in all places of His dominion. Give strength, then, to your understanding, and give wings to your imagination, and give holy fear to your heart while we try to enter upon those great matters "which eye hath not seen, nor ear heard, neither have entered into the heart of man. But God hath revealed them unto us by His Spirit."

When you try to do it, you cannot limit the presence of God to any one place on earth or in heaven—no, nor to all places on earth and in heaven taken together. Place, precinct, locality, situation—when you attempt it, you soon find how absolutely impossible it is to limit and restrict Almighty God in that way. Even to speak of His "house" in which we now are—and though Holy Scripture teaches us and encourages us so to speak—that is, all the time, to speak as a child, and to understand as a child, and to think as a child. Heaven and earth, time and eternity, all worship their maker in these adoring words and say: "Behold, the heaven, and heaven of heavens cannot contain Thee: how much less this house which we have builded."

Our more thoughtful men of science, in some of their profoundest speculations, try to penetrate to the true "constitution," as they call it, of the physical universe. But to us, God is the true and only constituent both of the physical and the spiritual universe. God is the ultimate analysis, and the innermost essence, and the deepest root, and the all-producing and the all-sustaining cause of all existence. The whole universality and immensity of all things, created and uncreated, is all one and the same mystery of godliness. All created things—the most firm and stable—would instantly stagger and reel back and dissolve into their original nothingness and annihilation if Almighty God withheld His all-upholding hand from them for one moment. The pillars of the earth are His, and it is He who has established the world on its strong foundations. From a grain of sand on the seashore up to all the endless systems of suns and stars in the heavens; from those creatures of God that are too small for the eye of man to see them, up to the choirs of cherubim and seraphim before the throne—to our ears they all unite and rejoice to sing, "In Him we live, and move, and have our being." "For of Him, and through Him, and to Him, are all things."

And then, if anything could add to the awe and the wonder of all that, it would be this all-transcending truth—that He who is everywhere is also *wholly* everywhere. Now that Almighty God is wholly and continually with every one of us in all the completeness and in all totality of His Godhead—what an absolutely bewildering thought is that! Absolutely bewildering were it not that it is revealed to us and is borne in upon us not to bewilder us but to enlighten us, and to support us, and to solace us, and to sanctify us, till it shall glorify us. Were we but able to receive it, we have our God, and the whole of our God, as much with us as if we had been Adam, new from the hand of God, and walking alone with the whole presence of God among the trees of the garden.

There is a certain far-off image and adumbration of all that even among ourselves. A father's presence with his children is not limited to one of them at a time. His fatherly presence is not broken up into so many portions and so distributed from time to time among his sons. And much less is a mother's love portioned and poured out according to the number of her sons and her daughters. Every one of her children has all their mother's presence with them, all her heart, all her thoughts, all her solicitude, all her prayers. Till, wheresoever she has a child, that child of hers can adopt the words of the great Psalm and say to his mother: "Whither shall I flee from thy presence? If I ascend up into heaven, thou art there: if I make my bed in hell, behold, thou art there.… If I take the wings of the morning, and dwell in the uttermost parts of the sea: even there shall thy hand lead me, and thy right hand shall hold me." Only—she might forget her sucking child, that she should not have compassion on the son of her womb: yet will I not forget thee.

But to come from God the Father to God the Son. What is this that God the Son here says to His disciples, and through them to us? "Lo," He says, "I am with you always, even unto the end of the world. Amen." And that, be it well remarked, just after He had said this also: "I ascend to My Father." And this: "I go to prepare a place for you." And this: "It is expedient for you that I go away." And this: "If ye loved Me, ye would rejoice because I said, I go unto the Father." And then, with all that, He actually says this self-contradictory-looking word: "Lo, I am with you always, to the end of the world. Amen." My brethren, you must never for one moment forget this. You must put out of mind and memory everything else in order at all times to remember this. This, namely—who and what He is who says to His disciples and to us these seemingly so contradictory things. Mark with all your might that it is not God the Father who says these so startling things—these, at first sight, so impossible-looking things about going away till the end of the world, and then in the next breath about remaining and abiding present all the time with men on the earth. It is not God the Father who says these strange things. Neither is it God the Holy Ghost. It is God the Son who alone so speaks. It is the Word made, and remaining, flesh. It is the God-Man. It is Immanuel, God with us. You have the whole key to this mystery of all mysteries, you have the complete reconciliation of all these contradictions and difficulties in your own tongue in which you were born. Even in this. "The only Redeemer of God's elect is the Lord Jesus Christ, who, being the eternal Son of God, became man, and so was, and continueth to be, God and man, in two distinct natures and one person for ever."

My brethren, if you would be wise yourselves to salvation and would make your children wise with you to their salvation, first learn with your whole mind and with your whole heart yourselves and then teach to your children "the truth as it is in Jesus." Talk about Him to your children when you sit in your house, and when you walk by the way, and when you lie down, and when you rise up. And thus taught of God the true mystery of God and of Christ, you will be able to reconcile into a glorious harmony of grace and truth all these so staggering speeches of your Lord and Saviour concerning Himself and concerning your salvation. And this is "the truth as it is in Jesus." This, that ever since His incarnation, ever since His birth of Mary, our Lord has possessed the nature of man in addition to, and in everlasting incorporation with, the Divine Nature. And thus it is that He sometimes speaks and acts in His Divine Nature and sometimes, again, in His human nature. Sometimes as pure Son of God and sometimes as pure Son of Man. As in these texts of this morning. As God the Son, He is with His disciples and with us everywhere, and wholly everywhere, and to the end of the world. Whereas, as He is man, He is no longer with His disciples, but is with His Father, and with the holy angels, and with the glorified souls of His saints in heaven. He no longer prays in Gethsemane and on His face and in a sweat of blood. He now stands a Prince and a Saviour, making all-prevailing intercession for His people at His Father's right hand. And it will only be when His office of intercession is for ever finished that the Word made flesh will appear on earth again, the second time, without sin and unto salvation.

You have it all wrapped up in these three unsearchable words: "two distinct natures." The one nature with all the infinite attributes of the Godhead belonging to it; and the other nature with all the finite and limited and located attributes of His true manhood belonging to it. And thus it is that such otherwise impossible blessings come to us out of His real and abiding and everlasting incarnation. For by means of His incarnation we have all the fullness of the Godhead bodily in Christ; and we have all that in a new and unspeakably blessed way. That is to say, we have the whole Divine Nature with all its Godhead attributes in Christ; and in Christ we have them all with that peculiar pity, and grace, and fellow-feeling added that come so home to Him and to us, through His possession and experience of our human nature.

> Though now ascended up on high,
> He bends on earth a brother's eye:
> Partaker of the human name,
> He knows the frailty of our frame.
> Our fellow-suff'rer yet retains
> A fellow-feeling of our pains:
> And still remembers in the skies
> His tears, and agonies, and cries.

And then, from all that, it follows that while His heavenly glory now and for ever endows His human nature to all its fullness; and perfects His human nature to every possible perfection; and crowns His human nature with every possible honour and reward; at the same time, all His heavenly glory does not remove or in any way obliterate or break down so much as one of the true borders and boundaries of His human nature. His divinity does not in heaven, any more than on earth, extinguish or in any way impair His real and true and ever-abiding humanity. He is now and He will for ever remain God and man in "two distinct natures and one person for ever."

To all eternity, and amid all his surpassing glory, we shall never need to say with Mary Magdalene: "They have taken away my Lord out of my knowledge, out of my sight, and out of my presence, and I know not in what light inaccessible they have again hid Him!" For to all eternity He will remain among us and one of us, the man Christ Jesus, the Lamb as He had been slain, only for ever crowned with the whole glory of God, as He is alone worthy to be crowned. Worthy is the Lamb that was slain!

1. A thousand thoughts crowd in upon our minds as we meditate on these majestic matters. One who meditated on these majestic matters from his fifteenth year, and that with a singularly original and adoring mind, has put his experience into these well-known

words: "My conversion made me rest in the thought of two, and two only, absolute and luminously self-evident beings—myself and my Creator." And again, in a great sermon: "To understand that we have souls is to feel separation from things visible, our independence of them, our distinct existence in ourselves, our individuality, our power of acting for ourselves, this way or that way, and our accountableness to Another for what we do. Till, in this way, we begin by degrees to perceive that there are but two beings in the whole universe, our own soul and the God who made it." Sublime, unlooked-for doctrine! Yet most true to every one of us!

2. But then, God is present and is wholly present only to him who believes that. Our belief does not indeed cause God to be; and our unbelief does not cause Him not to be. Only, this is His nature and our nature, that He is to each one of us just according as we believe Him to be. If we choose, we can say with the fool: "There is no God." Or if we choose, we can say with the saint: There is nothing else in the world but God and my own soul. Believe in God in His presence with you and His presence is immediately and wholly with you as it was with David in the Psalms, and with Jesus Christ in the Gospels, and with Paul in the Epistles. Have faith in God and in your own souls.

3. And then again, there is this. "There are three Persons in the Godhead: the Father, the Son, and the Holy Ghost; and these three are one God, the same in substance, equal in power and glory." That is to say, the three Divine Persons are wholly everywhere; they are all three wholly with you and me. Think of that! And think continually of that, especially in your prayers and praise. Sometimes turn to God the Father and say to Him, Father, I have sinned. Sometimes say to Him, Our Father which art in heaven. Sometimes, again say, Father, glorify Thy name. And sometimes say, Father of mercies, and God of all comforts. And sometimes just look up and say: Abba! Father!

Then again, while not turning away one moment from the Father, turn toward the Son and say: "Rock of Ages, cleft for me, Let me hide myself in Thee." And, again:

> Just as I am, without one plea,
> But that Thy blood was shed for me,
> And that Thou bidd'st me come to Thee,
> O Lamb of God, I come.

And then, at another time, and indeed continually, look up and salute the descending Comforter and say:

> Come, Holy Spirit, Heavenly Dove,
> My sinful maladies remove:
> Be Thou my guard, be Thou my guide,
> O'er every thought and step preside.

For they are "the same in substance, equal in power and glory."

4. My brethren, you speak in praise of a liberal education, and you consult as to where it is best to be found. You send one of your sons to study the Greek and Latin classics for the ennobling of his character, for the refining and the enriching of his mind, and for the peopling of his imagination with the great men and the great achievements of the greatest ages of this world's history. You send another to a different study for the strengthening and the disciplining of his reasoning powers. And another to a master under whose tuition he will form lifelong habits of observation, induction and classification. All well and good. And may all your anxiety and all your outlay be amply rewarded. Only, all the time, here is the most liberalizing and ennobling and refining and every way rewarding of all possible studies; and it is as open to the poor as to the rich, and to the old as to the young. Here is thought, infinitely the most magnificent; and observation the most inexhaustible; and experience, gathered out of God, and out of a man's own soul; out of all time, and yet to be gathered out of a coming eternity. Here is meditation, both the sweetest and the most strengthening. Here is the life of prayer on earth and the life of praise in heaven. Here is the chief end of our creation and our redemption—God. "That they all may be one: as Thou, Father, art in Me, and I in Thee. I in them, and Thou in Me: and that the love wherewith Thou hast loved Me may be in them, and I in them." Yes! What an education! What a sanctification! What a glorification is the practice of the omnipresence of God!

2

The Image of God

All that is within me, bless His holy Name (Psa. 103:1).
God said, Let us make man in our image, after our likeness …
So God created man in His own image (Gen. 1:26-27).

An image is any imitation, resemblance or similitude of another thing. An image is anything drawn, painted, sculptured or executed in any other way so as to resemble, repeat and reproduce some person or thing. We have the original and exact sense of the word sufficiently set forth in the second commandment of the Decalogue: "Thou shalt not make unto thee any graven image, or any likeness of anything that is in heaven above, or that is in the earth beneath, or that is in the water under the earth." This is the original and fundamental sense of the well-known word "image." But at the same time, such is the capacity and scope of the word that it can be and has been applied in a great variety of senses and put to a great variety of uses, artistic and ethical, material and spiritual, some of the highest and noblest of which I am now to attempt to elucidate.

1. By far the highest use and application of this word is made when the New Testament Scriptures apply it to the eternal generation and essential sonship of the second divine person. Though not set in as many words, the son-like image and similitude of the Son to the Father is sufficiently set forth in the dialogue between Jesus and the two disciples. Jesus said unto Thomas: "If ye had known Me, ye should have known My Father also, and from henceforth ye know Him and have seen Him." And afterwards to Philip: "Have I been so long time with you, and yet hast thou not known Me, Philip? He that hath seen Me hath seen the Father: and how sayest thou then, Shew us the Father."

And in as many words we have the apostolic doctrine of the divine image in an epistle: "God made all things by His Son, who is the brightness of His glory, and the express image of His person." And in another epistle the Son is described as the "image of the invisible God, the firstborn of every creature." And in yet another epistle we read of the glorious gospel of Christ, who is "the image of God." These passages are intended to carry us, if we have the mind to follow them, beyond and above and before creation. Here we see none, not the earliest and most exalted of His creatures. Here we are alone with God, eternal and immortal and invisible, who is before all things and by whom all things consist. And of that divine, eternal, and invisible life it is revealed and declared that the Son is the essential image of the Father. The only begotten Son is the image, though as yet the equally invisible image of the always invisible Father. The Son is the Father's image in nature or essence—in power, holiness, justice, goodness and truth, and in all other divine perfections. The Son indeed is such an image of the Father that he that seeth Him hath seen the Father. He that hath seen the Son hath no more occasion to say, "Shew me the Father." Indeed, with the most entire truth it may be said that the only-begotten Son of God is the Father in all divine attributes and perfections, in all things but personality and paternity—primal personality and fontal paternity. Athanasius, to whom the church of Christ owes so much, says: "The Son, being an offspring from the divine substance, is one in substance, Himself and the Father that begat Him. This is why what is said of the Father is said in Scripture of the Son also, all but His being called Father...." And Athanasius's latest and best editor adds: "Though the Son is in all things the Father's image, this implies some exception: for else He would not be like or equal, but the same.... Hence He is the Father's image in all things except in being the Father.... For the Son is the image of the Father, not as Father, but as God." This, then, in few words is the scriptural and ecclesiastical doctrine of the divine image in the eternal Son.

2. From this the highest, the almost too high use of the word "image"—from the heavenly use of an earthly word—I pass on the secondary use, the use made of the word in the text, "God created

man in His own image, in the image of God created He him." The first head dealt with the image of God in the eternal Son, and the second head deals with the image of God in man—in Milton's words, "in man, God's latest image."

According to the scriptural account of the creation of man there was in it a twofold act or process. "The Lord God formed man of the dust of the ground, and breathed into his nostrils the breath of life; and man became a living soul." The image of God in man is, so far, a complete and comprehensive likeness, but it is a likeness composed out of many features and laid down in many lineaments. There are many lines requisite to compose and complete the divine similitude. Now, in searching in man for the divine image, we at once pass beyond all in him that was "made of the dust of the ground." For no formation of dust, not even when it is refined and elaborated into flesh and blood—no such material substance can carry on it an impression of the image of God. It is not therefore in man's body, erect, noble, fair, beaming with intelligence and girded with strength as it is; it is not in man's body that the divine image stands, but in his soul, in his mind, in his conscience, and in his heart; or as we have from our youth been taught, the image of God in man "consists in knowledge, righteousness, and true holiness."

Let knowledge then be taken as the first of those features, those spiritual features in which we descry the presence of the image of God in man. Now, by knowledge that man was created with, it is not meant that man had from the first the faculty of acquiring knowledge, or the power of attaining and treasuring up the results of experience and contemplation. Man by nature had and has the power of observation, comparison, contemplation, consideration, and memory. But over and above that, he at first had possession of the best sources of knowledge in a more excellent way. Omniscience is one of the most clearly revealed attributes of the divine nature. God has knowledge of all things, as by direct and immediate vision of them. Now, though man in nothing shares this divine attribute, yet he had and still in measure has a gift, a creative gift, that in its way and measure may be said to partake of that divine prerogative. For in man as he came from the hand of God there was a rich and flowing fountain of innate knowledge. There was, as it were, a well of intuitional truth springing up continually in his mind and heart and conscience. Our father Adam left us this well as part of our impoverished inheritance. He drank of it himself, he and all his children; and in spite of all that has been done to choke and pollute it, it still springs up like living water in the deep and hidden places of the human heart. And this knowledge was not theoretical and speculative knowledge but a profoundly practical and immediately fruitful knowledge. It had its fountain and wellspring even more in the heart than in the understanding, in the conscience more than in the intellect. The heart of man, when God created it, entered into it and said: "This is my rest, here will I dwell." The human heart then was pure, and true, and good, and full of love. "God is love," and the image of God was best impressed on that which is the seat of love. Man's morning intellect was strong and clear above any intellect that has been possessed by any man since men's minds were darkened by sin. "Aristotle himself was but the rubbish of Adam." Man's intellect in Eden was clear and strong, and it was sweetened and made fruitful in all its parts and in all its operations by the purity and peace and gladness of his heart. The candle of the Lord shone on Adam's head. His body was the instrument and tabernacle of his soul; and his soul was the breath and, as it were, the very spirit of God Himself—so great was God's goodness to our race, and so excellent was His work of which it is said: "So God created man in His own image: in the image of God created He him."

It is a debate among scriptural students of human nature how much man lost of the divine image at the time of his fall—how much he lost and how much he still retains. To assist themselves first in discovering the truth about this matter, and then to assist them in discoursing on it to us, theologians have taken a distinction between what is losable in the divine image and what cannot be lost. There is first, say they, the natural image of God which, when once imprinted on the human soul, can never afterwards be obliterated or lost. Indeed, the natural image of God is not so much printed on the soul as incorporated with it. The very substance and structure of the soul is in the image of God. In the very spirituality of its substance the soul of man was and is and will for ever remain an image of God. The intellect, the power of reasoning and understanding; the will, the power of choosing, of accepting or rejecting; the conscience, the voice of a judge in our bosom—all these are natural, original, fundamental and inseparable powers and possessions of every human soul; and in these the substantial and, so to speak, structural image of God in the soul consists. The creature that has once come into possession of these features of the divine image can never again lose them. Wherever man is found—in Eden or in Sodom, in grace or in glory, in earth or heaven or hell—beneath all his good or evil, blessedness or misery, there will always be found a human mind, will, conscience. Indeed, sin and salvation, heaven and hell could have no meaning or even existence for a creature that had not so much abidingly within him of the original image of God.

Nowhere is the language in this truth so ably and eloquently set forth as in John Howe's *The Living Temple*. "The stately ruins," he says, "of this living temple still bear this doleful inscription over their portal—Here God once dwelt. Enough still appears of the admirable form and structure of the soul of man to show that the divine presence did sometimes reside in it, more than enough of vicious deformity to proclaim that He is now retired and gone. The altar is overturned and the candlestick is broken; and in place of the sacred incense, with its clouds of rich perfumes, there is a poisonous and hellish vapor continually rising up.... Look upon the fragments of that curious scripture that once adorned the palace of the great King; the lively prints of some undefaced truth, the fair ideas of things, the yet legible precepts that relate to practice....You come in all this confusion, on into the ruined palace of some great prince, and he that invites you to take a view of the soul of man says—Behold the desolation! Behold the ruins of the Fall! The faded glory, the darkness, the disorder, the impurity, the decayed state in all respects of this temple too plainly show that the great Inhabitant is gone."

3. The next step in our progress is to study the image of God in the Second Adam, the man Christ Jesus. We have already seen that He who in the fullness of time became the Second Adam had from all eternity been the divine Son, and as such the image of the eternal

Father. And moreover, such an image as that further revelations and manifestations of the Father were become possible through Him. In some way quite unfathomable to us, the divine nature had come nearer us and nearer all creation in the eternal generation of the divine Son. Creation and providence, revelation and grace had all become possible and indeed prophetic in the eternal Sonship. To borrow a modern philosophical notion and nomenclature—the unconditioned has become conditioned in the second person of the Godhead. "The Father in His monarchy and invisibility secures the majesty and invisibility of the Godhead in its secret place, while the Son, who issues thence, manifests its goodness and shows forth its beneficence; and hence the Father is the Son's incomprehensibility and invisibility while the Son is the Father's comprehensibility and visibility.... The Father is the invisible safeguard of divinity, in that He is its origin and fount; and the Son is the principle of its effusion, nay, the expenditure and emptying out of itself, saving always that the Father's inviolability is the Son's also, and the Son's accessibility and munificence is the Father's too. And hence it is that the Scriptures speak of the Father as invisible and of the Son as the image of the invisible Father; and hence the Scriptures sometimes say that God can be seen and sometimes again that He cannot be seen. The truth is, invisibility is reserved to the Father while visibility is undertaken by the Son."

"Before Abraham was, I Am," said our Lord, asserting His divinity and eternity. And so may we say in asserting the antiquity of the divine image in Him—Before Adam was "made" in the image of God, the eternal Son was "begotten" in that image. And hence as to one already with God, and one who is His fellow and counsellor and instrument, the Father said: "Let us make man in Our image and after Our likeness." And accordingly Adam was made after an older image of God than himself was, even as the Apostle says, "after the image of Him that created him." Thus it was that some of the church fathers called Adam a secondary and subordinate image, "an image of the image." And thus it is that in *Paradise Lost* we find "man" described as "God's latest image." And thus it became both possible and congruous that that divine person made man in His own image should restore that image when it was lost. And hence the fitness as well as the grace of the incarnation; hence his eternal preparation and predisposition, so to speak, for his economical offices of prophet and priest and king over and among the sons of men.

My brethren, it is no irreverent play upon words, but it is a most profound and fundamental truth to say that as Adam in his creation was made in the image of the Son of God, so the Son of God in His incarnation was in return made in the image of Adam. In His incarnation the Son took on Himself a created image of Himself when He took on our human nature. A body and a soul were prepared for Him—not, strictly speaking, as a new creation, but as a sanctified extraction and holy reproduction of the body and soul of Mary, which in this respect were just the body and soul of Adam. The body and the mind, the will, the heart, the conscience of the man Christ Jesus were all made in the image of Adam. The new creation that was begun in Christ, so far as it was a new creation, consisted essentially in this: in filling the Adamic mind that was found in Christ with divine light and divine truth; and in filling the Adamic will with filial humility and obedience; and in filling the Adamic heart with love to God and man, and the Adamic conscience with all the communion and peace of a holy and living temple. The image of God in Jesus Christ stood not in any new constitution or reconstruction of the human mind of fallen man, it stood rather in the Spirit of God preparing a human will and mind and heart with such a preparation as that the Son of God could dwell in them, and work through them, and make them an earthly temple for a season, and the heavenly temple for evermore. The image of God as seen in Christ the second Adam is simply a human understanding enlarged and enlightened without measure; a human will emancipated and carried captive under a sweet and blessed constraint to the will of God; a human heart which is a fountain of love to God, and grace to men; and a human conscience which lies in His bosom like a sea of glass before the throne of God.

4. I trust, my brethren, that in these deep and unfamiliar things we have not lost sight of our way or of one another. To make sure of that, let me repeat what we have learned. The first head dealt shortly, and

altogether inadequately, with the image of God in His only-begotten Son. The second head exhibited the image of God in Adam. And the third has just distinguished and displayed that same image as it is seen in Jesus Christ. And now, in the fourth and last place, I shall shortly speak of the image of God and Christ in regenerate men.

Regeneration means that return upon our first original, that happy return by redemption and renewal, by means of which, while remaining the same men we always were, we are yet carried back to the beginning and are, as it were, "born again." "Born again," that is, so as again to be made partakers; born partakers of those gifts and graces and privileges which had been received and lost before we were born. The New Testament speaks repeatedly and emphatically of our being "renewed after the image of Him who created us." Now, manifestly, to be renewed means that we receive again and become repossessed of something that we once had but have long lost. Now we know that the race of beings to which we belong possessed at first that very image of God which Christ now has, and after which we, the deformed and defaced children of men, are renewed again in our regeneration. The type, the normal type, was created once for all in Adam; and it is simply restored, ennobled, established, and perpetuated in Jesus Christ; and it is not so much created anew in each regenerate soul as it is individually and increasingly assumed or "put on." "Put on," says Paul, "put on the new man, which is renewed in knowledge after the image of Him that created him."

The regeneration is in the Scripture accounted far more glorious than the creation because there is in it a vastly greater display of divine power, and wisdom, and love. If there were less and more with the Almighty, it might well be said that it took far more power and wisdom to renew than to create a soul. At creation the soul was soft, pliant, ductile, impressible, responsive; the clay had not yet hardened into a "stony heart," and no such strange and supernatural instrumentalities were needed to create the soul after the image of God, no such instrumentalities of fear and hope, pain and sweetness, chastisement and comfort; and no such priceless labours as are represented by the cross and spirit of Jesus Christ. "You hath He quickened," exclaims the Apostle, "quickened by the same mighty power which wrought in Christ when He raised Him from the dead. Even when we were dead in sin, God hath quickened us together with Christ." And again to signalize and distinguish the grace of regeneration it is said, "which were born not of blood, nor of the will of the flesh, nor of the will of man, but of God." "And if children then heirs, heirs of God, and joint heirs with Christ"—predestinated and begotten of the Father to be conformed to the image of His Son.

And now, my brethren:

1. From all this let us learn first what I shall call a scientific or a philosophical lesson.

We must all have been struck as we looked upon nature, and read the daily increasing revelations of science—I say we must all have been struck with the human cast and character of all created things. All things seem as if they had been designed by a vast human mind and made by an all-mighty human hand. Every science in every one of its discoveries opens up more and more of the Adamic character of universal nature.

Indeed, science could open up nothing were it not that she follows the footsteps of a creator in whose intellectual image both the universe explored and the human explorer are each in their measure made. The divine creator, the whole creation, animate and inanimate, and the scientific student are all on one intellectual type and similitude. They all hold a fundamental likeness and a real intellectual relationship to one another. "God geometrises," said Plato. And every philosopher and scientific man might with equal piety and boldness claim the patronage and example of his maker in the same way. For who has not felt a thrill of wonder and surprise, immediately followed by a strangely familiar and home-like feeling, as he read that in the sun itself as in the farthest fixed stars the same chemical elements obtain, the same geometrical laws rule, and the same dynamical changes are continually taking place as in our own laboratories and workshops on the earth! Enlarged as his horizon has become, man is still the measure of all things; but he is so, and after all discoveries are made will still remain so, because he himself is made in the image of Him who made all things. Scriptural Christiology and natural science in all her departments must see eye to eye, must combine and co-operate before either becomes crowned and complete, since the one studies the creator of all things in His divine and human natures, and the other studies the creation, so full in all its parts, of a divinely-human, a God–man cast and character. The truth, here too, is in "Jesus."

2. The second lesson is one of a political, judicial, and social kind. "Whoso sheddeth man's blood, by man shall his blood be shed: for in the image of God made He man." And again, "The tongue is an unruly evil, full of deadly poison. Therewith bless we God, and therewith curse we men, which are made after the similitude of God." The prophets and the apostles here unite in holding up a shield over the assailed and insulted image of God in man. It is a species of deicide as well as murder to lift up our hand against our brother; and it is sacrilege as well as slander to speak evil of our neighbour. No price, according to these scriptures, no adequate price can be set on the life of the youngest child or the oldest man. The poor, the outcast, the incurably diseased, the stranger, the savage, as well as the newborn infant have all a claim upon us in which piety mingles with charity, and devotion to God with duty to man.

3. This doctrine of the divine image reads a lesson also against every hour of temptation. For every outward act of sin, every inward consent to sin, is another impious repetition of the first sin; and, like the first sin, is immediately followed by a fresh "fall." For every sin in a child of God strikes at the yet frail and insecure image of Christ in the soul; just as every act of sin in the unregenerate more effectually defaces the image of God still preserved in them. "Mortify, therefore, your members which are upon the earth.… Put off the old man with his deeds, and put on the new man, which is renewed in knowledge after the image of Him that created him."

4. Again, as "the things that are made" are a witness to all men concerning Him who made them; and as the incarnate Son is the express and visible image of the invisible and inaccessible Father, so all those who have put on Christ in their regeneration are images, illustrations and similitudes of Christ to those who have not otherwise seen Him. "He that hath seen Me hath seen the Father," said His express image. And if we were all that we ought to be we could

say the same: "He that hath seen us hath seen our Saviour." For every believer is in his own measure a visible image of his Invisible Lord. "Ye are the light of the world."

5. But if the history of the divine image in man is in many respects a humbling history, yet with all that, it has many cheering and sustaining and ennobling things to say to us; and I close this discourse with recalling to your thoughtful and adoring minds one of the chief: "We know that all things work together for good to them that love God, to them who are the called according to His purpose. For whom He did foreknow, He also did predestintate to be conformed to the image of His Son, that He might be the first-born among many brethren."

3

The Strappado

All my bones are out of joint (Psa. 22:14)

In old and evil days there was a diabolical instrument of torture in Spain called the strappado. And that cruel instrument was worked in this wicked way. The poor victim was first hoisted up to a great height by means of ropes and pulleys; and then he was suddenly dashed to the ground, till every bone in his body was torn out of joint and broken in pieces. And the name of the Spanish strappado has passed into the English language, because the old preachers of that day frequently employed the illustration of the strappado in their experimental sermons. As thus Goodwin: "Now his lusts, both of body and mind, do strappado a sinner's expectations. That is to say, his sinful imaginations hoist up his expectations of pleasure to a great height and then, suddenly, he is let fall. For when the sinner comes to enjoy his high expectations, they always prove themselves to be such flat and empty things that his soul, being completely cheated, says to itself: 'And is this all!' Thus always do a sinner's high expectations strappado him till his spirit is simply dashed to pieces within him."

So far as I know, the Spanish strappado was never imported into Scotland or England. But if we have not the scaffoldings and the pulleys and the ropes of that inhuman instrument among us, we have plenty of those personal experiences which are so vividly and so forcibly illustrated by those scaffoldings and pulleys and ropes and broken bones. For we have plenty of high expectations followed by deep disappointments; plenty of great and towering ambitions followed by great depressions; plenty of high hopes followed by low despairs; plenty seekings of great things for ourselves followed by small and heart-starving results. Till it has been powerfully impressed upon me that the Spanish strappado may have some important lessons to read to us in our own land and in our own day.

Well, to begin with: such are we, and such is this present life of ours, that lawful enough pursuits and lawful enough pleasures not seldom become our very worst strappados. As Goodwin says: "Pleasures that are quite lawful to us become altogether unlawful and unsatisfying when our affections and our imaginations are too frequently and too vehemently set upon them." There is no need for me to put a name upon such pleasures; every man's own conscience will name them to him. The sweetest and the most allowable thing on earth has become an absolute strappado to some men. I will not name it, lest you be not able to bear it. But all readers of Luther will remember that he is very bold about it and tells us his own strappadic experience of it.

Again, in a commercial country like ours, first the pursuit of wealth and then the possession of wealth strappados many men's souls. Many such men have lived to confess and say that when they were children they thought as children and understood as children. They thought, when they had attained to great wealth, how happy they would be. They thought that when once they had a great house full of vessels of gold and silver, with horses and carriages at their doors and troops of friends around their table, then it would be heaven upon earth with them. But when they became rich men, all those childish visions of perfect blessedness fled away. The Psalmist saw multitudes of such strappadoed men all around him in his day, and his lament over them was this: "Verily every man at his best estate is altogether vanity. Surely every man walketh in a vain show. Surely they are disquieted in vain. He heapeth up riches, and knoweth not who shall gather them." And our Lord also has this warning word to all such men: "Thou fool! This night thy soul shall be required of thee: then whose shall those things be which thou hast provided?" At the same time, there is no nobler pursuit on earth than the pursuit of riches if they are pursued in order that they may be spent on God and man, on the church of Christ and on His poor. The higher such men climb, the nearer heaven they rise; and they shall never know disappointment nor defeat. All success to all such men as work with their hands, or their heads, that they may have to give him that needeth!

On another side of human life, what a strappado the pursuit of praise and fame is to many men among us. Take this true illustration. A friend of mine, a minister in England, became absolutely intoxicated with the ambition to write a great book on a great subject. After years of neglect of his pulpit and his pastorate in his devotion to his book, he was in Edinburgh and called on me, and for hour after hour he poured out to me about his coming masterpiece. But when it came out, his book only received one little scurvy review in one obscure London newspaper. When I next saw my friend I scarcely knew him—so shrunk was he, both in body and in mind. He was like our text. He had had such a fall that all his bones were out of joint.

You will often see the same thing in preachers and public speakers. A member of Assembly, say, has laboured for weeks at a great speech which is to make his reputation. But when he enters the advertised hall, the house is empty. And he suffers such a fall from his pride that moment that he can scarcely command his strength enough to finish the fourth part of what he had written with such labour and such expectation. The pulpit also is the sure strappado of the popularity-hunting preacher. Even if he is puffed up for a time, the time soon comes for another to arise who wholly eclipses him, till he lies with broken bones at the foot of his forgotten and forsaken pulpit. The higher his ambition hoisted him up, the deeper and the more heart-breaking is his fall. Let these examples of strappado suffice. Every man whose eyes are open will see plenty of such examples all around him. And he is a happy man who is not such an example himself.

"God," says Goodwin, "had a whole book written about the strappado in Israel, and He employed King Solomon to be His penman in that pathetic book. No man was ever hoisted higher than King Solomon, and no man had ever a sadder fall. Just hear Solomon about himself in that matter 'I said in my heart, Go to, now, I will prove thee with mirth; therefore enjoy pleasure.… I sought in mine heart to give myself unto wine and to women.… I also made me great works: I builded me houses; I planted me vineyards.… I got me servants and maidens, and had servants born in mine house; also I had great possessions of great and small cattle above all that were in Jerusalem before me. I gathered me silver and gold.... I gat me men singers and women singers, and all the delights of the sons of men.... So I was great, and I increased more than all that were before me in Jerusalem.... And whatsoever mine eyes desired I kept not from them. I withheld not my heart from any joy.'" And so on, chapter after chapter.

Don't you envy Solomon? We all do. But Solomon's book is not yet finished. For, as we read on we come to this: "Then I looked on all the works that my hands had wrought: and, behold, all was vanity and vexation of spirit, and there was no profit under the sun. Therefore I hated my life, because it was all vanity and vexation of spirit. He that loveth silver shall not be satisfied with silver, nor he that loveth abundance with increase: this also is vanity. The sleep of a labouring man is sweet, whether he eat little or much; but the abundance of the rich man will not suffer him to sleep. Vanity of vanities, saith the preacher, all is vanity." The word strappado is not found in all the Hebrew Bible; but the thing was never better experienced and described than in the words of the preacher, the son of David, king in Jerusalem. Just read his bitter book for yourselves and see how full of lessons it is to you all, be you king or subject, labouring man or master, rich or poor, young or old.

There is not much that can properly be called gospel in Solomon's autobiography. At the same time the preacher was not left wholly without hope for himself and for men like himself. And what light there is in his dark book is all the brighter because of its so black background. For Solomon's own sake, we seize eagerly on such utterances of his broken heart as these: "I came to see," he says, "that wisdom excelleth folly, as light excelleth darkness." And again: "God hath made everything beautiful in its season: and it is God's will that every man should enjoy the good from his labour: and a man's labour, and his good from it, are the gifts of God to him." Again: "Better is an handful with quietness to enjoy it, than both hands full, with travail and vexation of spirit." Again: "Better is a poor man, if he is a wise man, than an old and foolish king who will not be admonished."

And this comes in about public worship, to which Solomon betook himself when he had learned the vanity of a life without religion: "Keep thy foot when thou goest to the house of God, and be more ready to hear than to give the sacrifice of fools. Be not rash with thy mouth, and let not thine heart be hasty to utter anything before God: for God is in heaven, and thou upon earth: therefore let thy words be few." Also: "When thou vowest a vow to God, defer not to pay it; pay that which thou hast vowed."

And with all his disappointments in life, Solomon was not so embittered as you would expect to see him. "Behold, it is good and comely for a man to eat and to drink and to enjoy the good of all his labour. Every man also, to whom God hath given riches and wealth, let him rejoice and enjoy his riches: for they are the gift of God." And again that beautiful passage: "Go thy way, eat thy bread with joy, and drink thy wine with a merry heart. Let thy garments be always white; and let thy head lack no ointment. Live joyfully with the wife thou lovest. And whatsoever thy hand findeth to do, do it with all thy might." Again: "A good name is better than riches." Again: "In the day of prosperity be joyful; but in the day of adversity consider." Again: "Cast thy bread upon the waters, for thou shalt find it after many days. In the morning sow thy seed, and in the evening withhold not thine hand." And then, that noble passage so nobly worded: "Remember now thy Creator in the days of thy youth, while the evil days come not, nor the years draw nigh, when thou shalt say, I have no pleasure in them. While the sun, or the light, or the moon, or the stars be not darkened, nor the clouds return after the rain; or ever the silver cord be loosed or the golden bowl be broken, or the pitcher be broken at the fountain; or the wheel broken at the cistern. Then shall the dust return to the earth as it was; and the spirit shall return to God who gave it." The preacher sought to find out acceptable words; and that which was written was upright, even words of truth. Let us hear the conclusion of the whole matter: "Fear God, and keep His commandments: for this is the whole duty of man." Happy he who has learned such wisdom as that out of all his liftings up, and castings down!

4

Look to Your Motives

If thine eye be single, thy whole body shall be full of light. But if thine eye be evil, thy whole body shall be full of darkness (Matt. 6:22-23).

Look at your motives! Our Lord says this to us over and over again in this chapter. Our Lord's words always go to the bottom of things. They always go to the bottom of our hearts. Our Lord's words are always quick and powerful and sharper than any two-edged sword, piercing even to the dividing asunder of soul and spirit, and of the joints and marrow; they are discerners also of the thoughts and intents of our hearts. Our Lord's words strip our hearts bare of all affectation and pretence, display and insincerity, ostentation and hypocrisy. "Thy word, O Lord, is very pure, therefore thy servant loveth it." "Search me, O God, and know my heart; try me, and know my thoughts. And see if there be any wicked way in me, and lead me in the way everlasting."

Our motives are the secret springs of our hearts. Our motives are those hidden things in our hearts that move us to speak and to act. Our lives all issue out from our hearts like so many streams out of so many deep and hidden springs, and thus it is that we are so often told in the Word of God to keep our hearts with all diligence. And thus it is that our Lord's teaching is so full of all the matters of the heart, and especially of the hidden motives of the heart. Take good heed of your motives, He says three times to us in this single passage. Be simple in your hearts, He says to us. Be sincere in your hearts. Be pure in your hearts. Be not men-pleasers. Be not eye-servants. Be not "hypocrites." Seek not to be seen of men. Seek secret places. Seek obscurity. Seek and keep silence. Do nothing for the praise, or for the approval, or for the rewards of men. Let not your left hand know what your right hand doeth. Live all your life in the presence of God. Lay open your heart to His eye alone. Seek to have praise of God. Work for His approval and for His reward who seeth in secret. "The light of the body is the eye: if, therefore, thine eye be single, thy whole body shall be full of light. But if thine eye be evil, thy whole body shall be full of darkness."

1. Now men alone, of all God's creatures on the earth, have motives. The sun and the moon and the stars all move. They all move with the motion which their Maker gave to them at the beginning, and which He continually conveys to them by His upholding and impelling hand. "In them hath He set a tabernacle for the sun, which is as a bridegroom coming out of his chamber. His going forth is from the end of the heaven, and there is nothing hid from the heat thereof." The fowl of the air also, the fish of the sea, all sheep and oxen also—they all creep, and walk, and run, and fly, each one of them after his kind—but it is never said of any of them that they have a motive in what they do or in where they go. They eat and they drink; they lie down and they rise up; but they never say: "When I awake I am still with Thee!" The ox knoweth his owner, indeed, and the ass his master's crib; but all the same, they cannot enter into their master's mind with them. They do what by bit and bridle he compels them to do; but with it all, they do not consider. They have no understanding. They have no power of the contrary choice. They were not made in their Maker's image. Their chief end is never said to be to glorify God and to enjoy Him for ever. They have all their appointed ends, and they all stand in the same ordinances in which they were placed at their creation; but they do not know their own ordinances nor who ordained them. To man alone God saw it good to give understanding—understanding, and conscience, and will, and a contrary choice. Alone of all things that live and move and have their being in God, man is moved by his own motives.

2. And thus it is that God goes down to our motives when He would know us altogether, and would discover us, and would conclusively judge us. We ourselves make every effort to get at men's motives when we would know them and would judge them. But we cannot wade with any security into that deep sea. Men's motives lie deep down beyond our discovery and jurisdiction. God's eye alone

can see and search out a motive. We all feel that we are not truly known till our motives are known. We all feel that we are not yet fully and finally judged till our motives are laid naked and open. I may do what seems to your judgement right or wrong, praiseworthy or blameworthy—but hold your peace about me till you are quite sure that you have all my motives laid out under your eye. When you praise me, you pain me and humiliate me if my motive was not a pure motive; and when you blame me, I appeal from your judgement to His before whose tribunal all my motives lie bare:

> For I am ware it is the seed of act
> God holds appraising in His hollow palm:
> Not act grown great thence as the world believes,
> Leafage and branchage vulgar eyes admire.

What I am in my motives, that I really am: that, just that, and neither more nor less. And it is the prerogative and glory of God to hold all my motives, "appraising them" in His righteous hand. "Talk no more so exceeding proudly," Hannah prayed and said, "and let not arrogancy come out of your mouth, for the Lord is a God of knowledge, and by Him actions are weighed." "God weigheth more," says Thomas, "with how much love a man worketh. He weigheth the motive more than the actual work. He doeth much in God's judgement who loveth much." And we all have by heart Paul's fine passage on motive under the name of charity in the thirteenth chapter of First Corinthians.

3. Now from all this, it follows as clear as day that our true sanctification, our true holiness of heart, our true and full and final salvation all lie in the rectification, the simplification and the purification of our motives. The corruption and pollution of our hearts—trace all that down to the bottom, and it all lies in our motives: in the selfishness, the unneighbourliness, the unbrotherliness, the ungodliness of our motives. We are all our own motive in all that we do. We are all our own main object and our own chief end. And it is just this that stains and debases so much that we do. It is just this that so pollutes our hearts in the sight of God; and it is this that makes all we do so polluted in our own eyes when we look at ourselves with the eyes of

God. It is this that makes so much of our very righteousness to be filthy rags; and it is this inward bondage to bad motives that makes all God's saints to cry out with Paul under their utter wretchedness. Our Lord's blessedness, amid all His labours and burdens and sorrows, arose out of this, that His motives in all that He did were good. His eye was single, and therefore His whole body was full of light. He pleased not Himself. He pursued not His own ends. He had all His motives outside of Himself and above Himself. He was always, even in His early youth, "about His Father's business." He worked for praise and for approval and for reward indeed—but it was never the praise or the reward of men, but always of His Father. And thus it was that He had a clean heart and clean hands and a clean and peaceful conscience in all that He did. And after His work was finished—because of the simplicity and the purity of His motives in all parts of His work—He had such a reception awarded Him in His Father's house as no other son or servant of God has ever had. Now, where our Lord was pure and perfect, we are still impure and imperfect. Where His eye was single, our eye is double. And where his body was full of light, our body, at its best, is but twilight and darkness. There are all degrees of purity and of impurity in our motives. But it is he whose motives are purest and whose eye is singlest who is most prostrated and humiliated and overwhelmed with the impure, selfish and ungodly mixtures of his own motives. In all he does, when he does his very best, in almsgiving, in fasting, in praying, in preaching and indeed in all his actions and words and thoughts—so deeply is it all infected with the deadly taint of himself that his motives are a constant source of self-despising, self-hatred and self-despair. And just as his Master will never be pleased with His disciple till all His disciple's motives are as pure as His own, so neither can the disciple of Christ ever be pleased with himself till he is pure as his Master is pure.

> Saints purest in God's eyes
> Are vilest in their own.

4. "The one thing needful," then, in all that we think and say and do is a good motive. The new birth that we must all every day

undergo, the one all-embracing change of heart that God demands of us and offers us in His Son every day, is a complete change of end and intention, a completely new motive. The fall of man took place when God ceased to be man's motive and man's end, and when each man became his own motive and his own end. And the supreme need of all men is just the restoration to their hearts of God as their true motive and their chief end. Every human heart cries with Augustine—every human heart in its own language: "Thou hast made me for Thyself, and I know no rest till I find my rest in Thee. Thou hast made us to be moved by one motive, and to be directed by one intention, and to rest with a perfect rest in one end; and both our motive and our intention and our rest are in Thee." "Capable we are of God," says Hooker in one of his magnificent passages—"capable are we of God both by understanding and by will. By understanding, as He is that sovereign truth which comprehendeth the rich treasure-house of all wisdom; by will, as He is that God of goodness, whereof whoso tasteth shall thirst no more.…Under man, no creature in the world is capable of felicity and bliss. First, because their chiefest perfection consisteth in that which is best for them, but not in that which is simply best, as ours doth. Secondly, because whatsoever external perfection they tend unto, it is not better than themselves, as ours is. How just occasion have we therefore, with the prophet, to admire the goodness of God! 'Lord, what is man that Thou shouldest exalt him above the work Thy hands'—so far as to make Thyself the inheritance of his rest and the substance of his felicity." "Whom have I," exclaims Asaph the psalmist—"whom have I in heaven but Thee! And there is none upon earth that I desire beside Thee. My flesh and my heart faileth; but God is the strength of my heart and my portion for ever."

5. Now, all serious-minded and self-observant men will surely say to all this that they know all this already and have long known it; they accept all this and delight to hear it; but the longer they live, the more they fail to attain to it. They see purity of motive and simplicity of end and directness of intention and godliness of life—all shining like the sun and the moon and the stars high up above them, so high above them that they despair of ever rising up to them. My brethren, be patient. Be instructed. The new heart of a saint of God has never

yet attained at a bound. A new life of motive and of disposition and of intention and of aim and end is not the growth of a day or of a year. All this present life is allotted by God to His saints to make them a new heart. This inward work will fill up your whole life to its last moment. God, till that moment, will work in you to will and to do, to rectify your motives and to protect and purify your ends to the last. Believe that, and the great work of your life is already half wrought. Believe what God's purpose with your life is. Lord, I believe. Help Thou mine unbelief! Believe nobly. Believe magnificently. Believe with Christ the greatest Believer and the chiefest Saint. Believe that all your life is laid out and filled up—not and never for any earthly and temporal end but always for a heavenly and an everlasting end! Not to give you rest and pleasure and satisfaction where those ends are not; but to give you, and to prepare you for, these ends where they alone are, where they are worthy of you, and where you will be both capable and worthy of them. Threescore years and ten, with all their deep providences, ordination from everlasting, searching exercises and subduing and weaning experiences of heart, means of grace, and foretastes of glory—are all not for one moment too much for the perfect sanctification and everlasting and secure salvation of an immortal soul.

Ask yourselves then, amid all those things divine and human, earthly and heavenly, outward and inward—ask yourselves if the one work of your life, the one undertaking and achievement of your life is making progress just in this question: "What is my motive in this that I now do? And in this that I now suffer? In the light of God, and under His eye, why do I do this and that? What is my motive? What is my intention? What is the end I have set before myself in this and in that?" And then we shall no longer be as the horse and the mule that have no understanding. We shall more and more set the Lord before us. We shall say in every enterprise, What would my Master have me here to do? And we shall answer ourselves: "O Lord, I am Thy servant. I am Thy servant and the son of Thine handmaid. Thou hast loosed my bonds!" At the same time, it is by no means necessary to torture ourselves and to be in continual bondage to the letter of the law. We do not stop at every step of a journey and ask ourselves what place we are going to and why we are going to that place. We weigh our motives well before we start, and if they are right we set out; and if they are not right, we turn back. But once having made up our mind and started, we go on, enjoying the way, conversing about many things by the way, refreshing and resting ourselves by the way, and setting out again on our journey. And let the love of our heart be once rightly placed; let our treasure once be in heaven; let our motive once be God and our neighbours and not ourselves; and with many halts and many hungerings and thirstings, with many stumblings and falls even, yet our faces are still steadfastly set to the end of our journey; and the path of the just will lead us at last to our journey's end. Walking under the finger-post of the golden rule, walking in the light of a single eye and a right intention, we shall more and more walk at liberty, till all we think and all we do is pleasing in God's eyes.

1. Now from all this there follow two or three plain lessons. And this very plain lesson to begin with—that we cannot, by any possibility, know, so as to judge, our neighbours' motives. God has not given us the ability. He has reserved that divine ability to Himself. And at his peril, therefore, let a man intermeddle with another man's motives. Every human being holds secrets in his heart that the day of judgement shall for the first time publish abroad. Every human being holds in himself a whole world of mystery to all his fellows; and most of all to those who know him best. Attempt to judge no man's motives, then, for you cannot do it. You are a wise man and a true man and a good man if you can judge your own, and yourself on account of them. Judge yourself, then, and you shall not be judged; but judge other men, and with what measure you mete it shall be meted out to you again. Leave all judgement of other men's motives therefore to the Judge of all the earth—to Him Who will judge you and all men by the thoughts and the intents of the heart.

2. Again, it is surely a great comfort to a good man to know that a good motive makes the smallest act both great and good in God's heart-searching sight. Splendid deeds that are blazoned abroad by a thousand trumpets are but "splendid sins" in God's judgement, unless they are done out of a secret motive of true and genuine goodness. Unless love to God and to man, unless self-forgetfulness and

self-conquest lay at its root, the most far-sounding deed that ever any man did was but dust and ashes and far less than that in the sight of God. Whereas one single cup of cold water, one visit, in passing the door, to a sick-bed, a salutation on the street, a shaft of love and honour and goodwill shot in secret over the city or over the sea, for love's sake and for Christ's sake: "Come, ye blessed of my Father: inherit the Kingdom prepared for you!"

3. And to come back to this chapter for our last lesson: three times it is told us—and it must therefore be a lesson of the last importance to us to learn—three times over our Lord says of the Pharisees: Verily, I say unto you, they have their reward. Verily, I say unto you, they have their reward. And the third time: Verily, I say unto you, they have their reward. And then, over against that, our Lord says to His disciples, and through them to us: "Give all your alms in secret; fast and pray in secret; seek out secret places and hide yourselves and all that you do with your Father in secret; and your Father which seeth in secret will reward you openly. And blessed are ye when men, not knowing your good motives, shall revile you and persecute you and shall say all manner of evil against you falsely for My sake." As much as to say: Go down, if need be, to your grave unknown and undiscovered, hated, despised, misjudged, misrepresented, misunderstood; only keep your heart hidden with Christ in God. And when Christ, who is your life, shall appear, then shall ye also appear with Him in glory!

5

The Individual and His Salvation

Work out your own salvation (Phil. 2:12).

Alexander Vinet in his exquisite *Studies in Pascal* has this: "I place high up," he says, "among the traits that make Pascal's character so eminent, his intense individuality; I place high up his great, singular, and outstanding gift of always being himself, his high distinction of having thoughts and principles and experiences of his own. Pascal stood upon his own feet if ever man did. His philosophy and his religion and his literature had their roots deep down in himself, and not in another."

And what Vinet says so excellently of Pascal is true, in its measure, of every man—of every man, that is, who is a man at all. We all have our own individuality. It may not be so intense as Pascal's; it may not be so commanding; it may not be of such depth and such strength; but we all have our own individuality, great or small, rich or poor. "In a great house there are not only vessels of gold and of silver, but also of wood and of earth"—and you are one of those vessels. In every great building also there are foundation stones and copestones; stones laid away out of sight in the earth and other stones that shoot up and shine in the sun; lintel-stones, and pillars, and pinnacles; there are corner-stones and there are stepping-stones—and so on. And you are one or other of those stones.

In a body, also, there is the head and there are the feet; there are the arms with the hands; there are the eyes and the ears; and some parts are comely, and some parts are less comely. And you are one of those comely, or less comely, parts. In short, you are yourself, and not another. And the wisdom of your life, and the success of it, will be to discover and to know yourself. "The sounding-line," to borrow a phrase again from Vinet—"the sounding-line that reaches down to any man's true and proper self is not easily handled—it is not easily let down: it is not easily drawn up, and it is not easily read and recorded: it is not easily handled, and it is not pleasant to handle it, so dark, so double, so full of weeds and tangles is the bottom of the inward sea of self—so absolutely abysmal are the depths of each man's own individuality."

To begin with:

1. You are yourself, and not another in your *sin*, says this great text, by implication if not in as many words. Even in that universal sinfulness which you share with all mankind you are absolutely yourself. "Original sin" is that corruption and pollution, that debasement and destruction, of human nature which we have all inherited from our fathers, and which we transmit to all our children. Some men inherit a larger share of human nature than others, and with that far more of the corruption of human nature. Some men are small and slight, poor and incapacious in their natures; and their original sin is as their natures are. Other men are great men, powerful men, massive men, giants standing among dwarfs, lions and tigers standing among moles and mice. Some men have all a lion's strength in their sin, and some all a tiger's cruelty and bloodthirstiness. When they sin, it is like a hundred men all sinning at once; and when they repent, they melt all our hearts to tears. We all are in our human nature just as God has seen it good to make us; but, great or small, giants or dwarfs, oaks in the forest or the gourds of a night—we are all full of sin: we are all "made of sin," as Andrewes has it; and all that sin, great or small, is our own. "My sin is ever before me," sobbed out a gigantic sinner. "I am the chief of sinners," agonized another great man and great sinner. "In me," he said to God's saints in his day, when he was under the sounding-line of God's sanctification—"in me there dwelleth no good thing." And you all are yourselves, just as much as David, or Paul, or Pascal, or Andrewes, or any great sinner of them all. You are not of their size. You are not of their immense mental or spiritual measurement. You can neither sin nor repent like them. Sin and repentance like theirs would consume you on the spot. A night like one of David's nights would turn you to dust and ashes before

the morning. But you are what you are, and what you have made yourself. Your past life is your own; your present heart and character are your own; your future intentions and purposes and resolutions are known only to yourself and to no other man.

2. And just because your sin and your sinfulness are so absolutely your own, so will your *salvation* be. One of the surest signs that your salvation is at last begun and well on is your unshakable conviction that, as to sinfulness, you are alone in the whole world and have no equal, no fellow, and no near neighbour. And that sense of aloneness and unapproachableness and monstrosity in sin will grow upon you as you grow in grace in the intelligence and individuality of grace. The truth is: it is only when you begin to work out your own salvation in right earnest that you will discover what great men mean when they speak and write about individuality. Pascal was by nature a great man, one of the greatest of the sons of men; but after he became a subject of grace, after his conversion, he became an immensely greater man and an immensely more individual man. In depth and in grasp of mind, in nobleness and in superbness of mind, in the magnificence of the things he now conversed with, and in the grandeur of his ways of conversing with them, Pascal was altogether a new man. Life and death, redemption and salvation, grace and truth, sin and righteousness, holiness and eternal life, God and man and Jesus Christ, became ever-growing realities, and everything else to be dreams and vanities to Pascal. Before his conversion, Pascal was but one of his own miraculous and mathematical machines; but as his salvation went on, so did his intellect, and his imagination, and his conscience, and his heart, and his whole individuality. And so, in your measure, it has been with you. You are now a new creature. You belong to a new race of God's creatures. You have been born again. All things have become new to you. The eyes of your understanding have been opened and anointed. You walk on the earth with God. Your conversation is held with God's saints. Your conversation is in heaven from whence you look for your Saviour. And now, ever since, how you work at your own salvation! What a salvation you now need! And what a Saviour! What a Bible also, and what preaching! Who is sufficient to divide out the Divine Word henceforth to you?

What a Benjamin's mess you could sit down to at every Sabbath and still say, Give, Give! What prayers you now offer, and say Amen to them! What strange, what guilty reading you go through in your secret place when your house is asleep! Truly, old things are passed away with you! You are indeed a wonder to many! Only, go on: go on and on in your salvation, in your so secret life, in your life so hidden with God. Only go on, and you shall surely achieve and attain in the end. You have no fellow and no companion and no helpmeet here. But in your Father's house there are many mansions. And He is surely preparing a place for you. Since He has taken your heart so captive that you cry to Him night and day, "Whom have I in heaven but Thee?" surely He will not leave your soul in hell, nor always suffer one who loves holiness like that to lie down at the last in the pit of corruption! Surely no! Surely no!

3. "For"—to proceed—"it is God that worketh in you both to will and to do."

What a revelation! What a thing to say! What a thing for any man to believe to be true about himself! What a magnificent life is the life of salvation! What grace! What glory! What surpassing blessedness! God! God Almighty! His very Self, and not another, working in us! Working immediately, and with His very own hands in us! Awake, thou that sleepest! "When I was a child, I spake as child, I understood as a child, I thought as a child: but when I became a man, I put away childish things." Surely! Who would not? For what a workshop, what a laboratory, what a forge, what a crucible is the soul of man, and my soul! What living materials to be wrought upon, and what living tools to work with! And what a Workman enters my soul, goes up and down in my soul, takes all those tools and instruments into His hands, and turns them in upon my soul to its salvation! What a master-workman working in us, and we working in our own souls under Him! And our souls all the time the workmanship and the everlasting output of God, and of ourselves under God. That, then, is God! That is God, and no man ever told me! That is not chance, or accident, or mood of my own mind: that is not a man, or a man's book, or a minister's sermon acting on me! That is God with all those tools in His hands. That is God at His God-like work of making me to will and to do; making me willing and able to pray, to repent, and to reform; making me willing and able to think, to stop and consider, to open my eyes, to look behind and before, to take that right step, to stop and take back that wrong step, to enter my own soul and to see what still lies to be done by me in my own soul,to stand no more idle, to work while it is day—seeing the night cometh when no man can work.

My heart and soul, then, is the work-stuff, the work, and the workshop of God, and I knew it not! No one ever took me and told me. And I had almost misunderstood and missed my own and individual salvation altogether! What were my tutors and my governors, my preachers and my pastors, my father and my mother all the time thinking about, and I unsaved! And I on their hands, and did not know the very meaning of the word salvation; nor how to picture it myself, nor where it was worked out, nor under what master-workman! But while once I was blind, now I see. That is God! Now! That is God at His work within me. That blow of His hammer that has broken my hard heart! That stroke of His axe at the root of my life! That plunge of His pruning-knife! That furnace seven times heated! That overthrow, that shipwreck, that utter desolation, that hope that now maketh me all my days ashamed! That so bitter cup to wean me from all the cups of earth, since when I have drunk on earth the cup of heaven! And without ceasing, God works, as the psalmist discovered God in his day, and in his own soul. The everlasting God!—He neither slumbers nor sleeps, sang David in one of his so divine and so individualistic psalms. And He is the same today. Absolutely without ceasing He works. He visits us in our very dreams, does He not? And our reins instruct us in the night seasons, do they not? As if He had no other man's salvation on His hands but ours! We see, we hear, we taste, we feel Him and His work in us every day and every night, and every hour and moment of the day and night.

"To will and to do." To have us hew down that dead tree under His direction. To have us plant deep under His direction that living root. To lay the living plummet to that living wall. To lay in living mortar that living stone. To plane a living plank here, and to fix in a living nail there. To make such and such a call on our neighbour, an errand or a call of reconciliation, and repair, and recognition, and reception; to write such and such a letter of love; to send such and such a sanctified and sanctifying gift; to make such and such a sin-pardoning apology and redress; to deny ourselves such and such a self-indulgence; to take up, without a whisper of complaint, such and such an everyday cross; to redeem such and such a time for prayer, and so on—in short, to work out, without ceasing, our own salvation—God, all the time, working in us both to will and to do.

4. Now, with all that going on within me, you come to me with your snares and your seduction, with your offers and your invitations. Come with us, you say. Join with us, you say. Share with us. Cast in thy lot among us. Be one of us. Put away thy scruples, you say. Do not be a puritan. God is love. God is the Father of all. God is not a hard master. You know the way that men speak. You know with what softness and with what self-indulgence some men take their salvation. You have heard it all before. You were well-nigh lost by hearing it, and giving ear to it. No—you say with all civility, but with a great firmness: No! I cannot come. The salvation of my soul is precious to me, and I dare not endanger it. I have made up my mind. I have made my choice, and you must not tempt me to turn back. "Explain Vinet's words, 'The piety of Pascal was a *passion*.' Compare Paul's words, 'Yea, what *carefulness* it wrought in you; yea, what *clearing of yourselves*; yea, what *indignation*; yea, what *zeal*; yea, what *revenge*.' Compare this also out of the *Serious Call*: 'Unless our *passions* are bent on our salvation we shall scarcely be saved.'"[1] We are working out our salvation in our classes this very week by the study and the practice of such questions as these.

5. The Apostle Paul was Greek scholar enough, and preacher and pastor enough, and experienced Christian man enough to choose his words well. And he accents and emphasises and underscores and strengthens his words in the text in every possible way. Work out your own salvation, he says, with a weight and a solemnity that we do not fully feel in the English. Work it out to the very end, he wrote to the Philippians; and they, with their quick, new-born intelligence,

---

[1] This was an extract from the notes which Dr. Whyte had given to his classes to guide their studies for the week.

took up his passionate appeal in all its truth and power and impressiveness. Never stop working at your salvation, he writes. Never fall asleep at it. Never say that you have attained and are already perfect, else you are no converts, and will be no crown of mine! Never say that your calling and election are sure. Stand fast: and having done all, stand still fast. Endure to the end. Work on at your own soul, while a spot or a speck, a taint or a tarnish of sin is left in your soul. "The perseverance of the saints is made up of ever new beginnings." No. There is no fear of any true converts of this Apostle saying that they are already perfect. The chief fear is that they who work hardest at their own salvation should come to give it up through despair. But they must not. That is not to be despaired of surely—that which God has on His hands and on His heart. And of all the things He has on His hands and on His heart, there is nothing so near to His heart and so tied to His hands as the salvation of that man who works without ceasing at his own salvation. Be not too much discouraged then—O thou worker!—at such a discouraging work! Do not despair. Do not throw down the slow work in disgust and despair. Work on at it. Work it out, for it is God which worketh in you to will and to do. And, I am persuaded that neither death nor life, nor things present nor things to come, shall be able to separate you from the love of God, which is in Christ Jesus our Lord. Work on then, till God Himself shall make perfect that which concerneth you.

6

The Element of Time in Our Devotions

What, could ye not watch with Me one hour? (Matt. 26:40).

Our Redeemer was in the Garden of Gethsemane. His hour was come. He knew that His agony was fast approaching Him, and He felt as if He would be strengthened somewhat if He had two or three of His disciples near Him. But no! Even that slight support was to be denied our Saviour in that awful hour. His three chosen disciples were within a stone's-cast of the scene of His agony; but then, they were all three fast asleep, that the Scripture might be fulfilled—"I have trodden the winepress alone, and of the people there was none with Me." Their master did not arm the seventy and set them to defend the garden gate. He did not ask the eight, even, to do more than just to sit down and wait inside the garden gate, to see what the end of that midnight would be. And He only asks Peter and James and John that they shall stay within earshot of Him for "one hour," and shall keep awake for His sake. Nay—so little exacting is their master that lonely midnight, that if Peter alone will "watch" with Him, He will be satisfied. If He had returned and found Peter on his knees when He Himself rose off His face in a sweat of blood—the sight of Peter so employed would have been more to Peter's lonely Master than an angel from heaven strengthening Him. But as it was—when He came to Peter, He found that disciple three times fast asleep. Peter! who had protested at the table, only an hour before, that, as for him, he would die with his Master.

Now "all these things happened to them for ensamples; and they are written for our admonition on whom the ends of the world are come." And it is not for nothing, you may depend upon it, that our Lord here lays such pointed stress on "one hour's" watching and praying that night in Gethsemane. I do not think it is possible for any of His true disciples, among ourselves, to read this solemnising Scripture without having his conscience struck sore with that rebuking word—"one hour"—that night of our redemption. Yes, you may depend upon it: this remonstrance here addressed to Peter has been recorded not for his sake alone, but for our admonition and instruction also.

But there is a previous question even to that—and it is this: Are we, at all, the manner of men to whom the remonstrance of the text is likely to be addressed? For our Lord by no means addressed this remonstrance to all His disciples that night. By no means. He had many good and true disciples, in Bethany and in Jerusalem, to whom He said nothing about watching and praying "one hour" with Him that night. He only asked Peter and James and John to do that. He did not even ask the eight in the distance to watch and pray. He simply bade them sit down and wait for Him and for the three. The eight in the distance were good and true disciples; but then they were only ordinary men. They were, comparatively speaking, commonplace men in their personal religion and in everything else. But the chosen three, on whom that "hour" of watching and prayer was laid that night, they were far from being ordinary men, or men with a commonplace call. James, the brother of John, was foreordained to fall under Herod's murderous sword almost immediately. And that hour in the neighbourhood of his Master's agony, and one hour, more or less like it, every night after it, would have prepared James for his martyrdom as nothing else could possibly have prepared him. And like James, *you* may have some martyrdom of some kind soon to come upon you. And that late hour every night, which you are at present wasting on unnecessary sleep, or in worse ways, may be the only thing that can possibly prepare you for what is fast coming upon you. Peter, again, was Peter. And if any man in all the discipleship of that day needed to watch and pray, it was surely Peter. You know what manner of man Peter was. He was full of all kinds of capacities and possibilities. There was simply nothing that Peter might not live to do, once he was made ready to do it. But he was not ready yet—not by a long way. No, nor will ever be ready, without many a midnight of watching and prayer. Peter, like ourselves, is full of the warmest words—on occasion. Now vowing away his life at the Lord's Table; and then, before the cock crows, denying the Lord that bought him. Above all things, Peter needed that hour of prayer that night, and, neglecting it, turning it into sleep, his temptations and his opportunities, all that night and all the next morning descended upon him, and found him utterly unprepared to meet them. Now *you* may be another Peter in our day; and if you are, one hour alone with Christ every night will be the making of you; and nothing else will.

Or again, you may be more like John. You may be a man of a meditative, mystical, spiritual mind. Now if that is the nature of your mind, it will never come to its best out in the world, keeping late hours with the men and women of the world. With such a rare mind as yours is, you must be much at home and much alone; and when you are alone you must be religiously and spiritually and devotionally occupied. In no other way will you ever come to full height of your high calling.

But on the other hand, if you are, and are always to be, just an ordinary disciple; if you are to be only one among many; if you are content to remain characterless and unrecognisable among the multitude; then you may, with the multitude, escape Gethsemane and all its late and lonely hours of watching and prayer. Only, make up your mind, and count the cost. For, in that case, escaping the preparation, you must not expect to be found able ever to suffer much, or to do much, in any way, for Jesus Christ and for His Church in this world. And if you do not suffer with Him, you must not expect to reign with Him.

Now a *whole hour*, it must be admitted, is a long time. But it is not so much the length of time: it is rather this—that we really do not know what to do with ourselves for a whole hour. We are like Santa Teresa. She made use of a sandglass; and she tells us, in her autobiography, how she used to glance at the glass to see if it was not nearly run down yet, so that she might escape out of her place of prayer with a good conscience. Now, like Teresa, we have it on our conscience that we ought to be alone with ourselves, and with God, for some decent length of time every night; but then, there is no hour of all the twenty-four that goes so slowly, and that hangs on our hands so heavily, as just the hour of secret prayer. So much is that the case that it is an immense service done to us when any author, or any preacher, directs us how to get that dreary and guilty hour filled up, so as to make it somewhat less of a task, somewhat less of a torture.

You might try this. You might begin by cutting down the hour. If a whole "hour" is too long for you, take half an hour; or even to begin with, take a quarter. Christ is not a hard taskmaster. He will not bind you to a hard-and-fast bargain—if you are unwilling. And besides, you can get through a great deal in half an hour; or even in a quarter of an hour. You can name a great many forgotten people, and a great many forgotten things, in half an hour or even in a quarter. You can go over your past day in a rough way in much less than an hour; in very much less, if you are in a hurry.

Then again, there is this to lighten and alleviate the strain. You do not need to lay it on your conscience that you must be on your actual knees all the time. Not at all. Rise up. Walk about the room. Go out and look up at the stars. Say, "What is man that Thou art mindful of him?" Come in again. Sit down. Take help out of Andrewes, or another. Lift up your hands. Lift up your eyes. Recite a promise. Chant a psalm. Say over an Olney or a Wesley Hymn to yourself. Do anything you like. Prayer is the most elastic exercise possible. Communion with God has no hard-and-fast rules and regulations. And if at the end of the half-hour you are beginning to have some liberty, and possibly to feel some delight—*go on*. You have still another half-hour before you. Never mind the clock striking. Tell it to strike loud for those who should be home by this time in their beds. Say to it as Teresa said afterwards, "Strike on, for by thy striking thou art but telling me that I am another hour nearer my heavenly Bridegroom!"

Then there is your Bible to help you fill up your hour. And once you have begun, really, to read your Bible—one hour each night will be far too short. You will forget hours and everything else many a night over your Bible—once you have begun to read it to yourself alone. The Psalms, for instance. The best of the autobiographic and experimental Psalms were written late at night, and when the Psalmists were alone with God. And they were written, so they must be read. And then, the Gospels. And after them, the Epistles.

Take your Bible, then, to help carry you through your hour of prayer. And as you sit down, say, "Come, my Lord, for I have an hour free tonight for Thee, and for my own soul." And I will promise you that you also will soon have proved it true, "My soul shall be satisfied as with the marrow and fatness: and my mouth shall praise Thee with joyful lips, when I remember Thee upon my bed, and meditate on Thee in the night watches."

Then again, there is this well-approved way of filling up the hour, and of giving an intense interest to it:

> Let not sleep come upon thy languid eyes,
> Before each daily action thou hast scanned.
> What done; what left undone; what done amiss.
> From first to last examine all; and then,
> Blame what is wrong, in what is right rejoice.

Now if a pagan philosopher, whose lot was cast by God's providence five centuries before Christ, practised that self-scrutiny for an hour every night, and taught the devout habit to all his disciples, what manner of person in that matter ought we to be? That was Pythagoras. And Xenocrates also, Diogenes tells us, used to meditate with himself several times a day, and always allotted one hour of each night to silence.

As we have seen, their Master did not expect all His disciples to watch with Him that night; but He did ask and He did expect Peter and James and John to do so. And in like manner, there is one class of people among us who should have no difficulty in filling up their one hour every night of watching and prayer. "Hast thou considered my servant Job?" the Hearer of prayer asks of all fathers and mothers among us. For when Job's sons and daughters were invited out to a supper and a dance, did Job go to sleep, do you suppose, at his usual hour, and with his usual repose of mind? Far from that. For what do we find written concerning Job, for our learning? We find this. As soon as Job's children had started off in their gay clothing and in their high spirits, their old father that moment went out to his flock and took a lamb according to the number of his sons and daughters, and offered sacrifice for them all to God. "For who knows," he said, "what temptations my children may meet with before they return home?" And then he sprinkled the atoning blood in the direction of the house of feasting, and ceased not from his intercessions till he saw his children home at sunrise—if the suppers in the land of Uz lasted so long. And not on their nights of late hours only, but every night, as our children grow up around us—what a privilege, what an absolute necessity, it is for a father and a mother to have an hour set apart in which to reflect, and to plan, and to pray concerning their children. You might do this, my friends, an hour every night. How many children has God given you to bring up for Him? and what are their names? and at which ages have they arrived? You might take Susanna Wesley's way. She took Jacky apart one night, she tells us—and Charles another. And her two boys are now known to all the world as John and Charles Wesley. And she read and prayed both "with and for" her whole family an hour each night. And when they were old enough, they shared their mother's work among the younger children. You might begin to do something like that; and who can tell how God would pay you your wages? The hour may hang heavy on other people's hands. It cannot possibly hang heavy on a parent's hands. Go over, towards God, the things in your children that are causing you anxiety. The things that, if they go on, will yet bring down your grey hairs with sorrow to the grave. As also, go over the things in yourself that are destroying your influence with your children. "I will behave myself," said the Psalmist, "wisely in a perfect way. O when wilt Thou come to me? And I will walk within my house with a perfect heart."

Whoever you are—parent or child, old or young, sinner or saint—give yourself to prayer. Let no distaste for prayer turn you away from it. Let no want of practice, let no difficulty in it, make you give it up in despair. Let no greatness of sin, or frequency of sin, frighten you away from the Throne of Grace.

Begin tonight; and never, on any account, give it over. Whatever else you do, or do not do—in God's name I beseech you to pray. Pray, and you will pray yourself into a life of pardon and holiness, till you pray yourself into heaven itself. And *begin tonight*. Only try one week of it, and then judge for yourselves.

7

A Wonder in Heaven

There appeared a great wonder in heaven (Rev. 12:1–5).

A wonder is something that arrests, and surprises, and astonishes. A wonder is something unexpected, unprepared for, unprecedented, and surpassing all our experience. The whole world is full of wonder to a child. "When I was a child, I spake as a child, I understood as a child, I thought as a child: but when I became a man, I put away childish things." But the Apostle put away the wonders of his childhood, only to be taken possession of by far greater wonders; till, in the ripe manhood of his mind and heart, he is not able to put words upon the wonders he has seen. "Whether in the body, or out of the body, I cannot tell: God knoweth—such an one caught up to the third heaven. How that he was caught up into paradise, and heard unspeakable words, which is not possible for a man to utter."

1. "I saw a great wonder in heaven," says John also. But before we come to that, heaven itself is a great wonder. Just heaven itself. Heaven is the seat and centre indeed of wonder. Wonder has her very throne and empire in heaven. Heaven is the true wonderland. Everything that is really wonderful, everything that surpasses, everything that captivates, everything that enthralls, everything that transcends—it is all collected into heaven. Even to paint a far-off picture of heaven, prophets and apostles have been compelled to lay this whole earth under contribution, for forms and colours, for riches and beauty, wherewith to delineate and adorn their theme. As thus: "For brass I will bring gold, and for iron I will bring silver. Violence shall no more be heard in thy land, wasting nor destruction within thy borders: but thou shalt call thy walls Salvation, and thy gates, Praise. The sun shall no more be thy light by day, neither for brightness shall

the moon give light unto thee, but the Lord shall be thine everlasting light, and thy God thy glory. Thou shalt no more be termed Forsaken, neither shall thy land be termed Desolate, but thou shalt be called Hephzibah, and thy land Beulah."

And then, the New Testament seer has this splendid passage on this same subject. "And I, John, saw the Holy City, New Jerusalem, coming down from God out of heaven, prepared as a bride adorned for her husband ... having the glory of God. And her light was like unto a stone most precious, even like a jasper stone, clear as crystal. And the city was pure gold, like unto clear glass. And the twelve gates were twelve pearls; every several gate was of one pearl, and the street of the city was pure gold, as it were transparent glass. And he shewed me a pure river of life, clear as crystal, proceeding out of the throne of God, and of the Lamb. And the throne of God and of the Lamb shall be in it, and His servants shall serve Him. And they shall see His face, and His name shall be in their foreheads." And more than all that. For it is written that "Eye hath not seen, nor ear heard, neither have entered into the heart of man, the things which God hath prepared for them that love Him."

2. But the "great wonder" that John saw in heaven was not heaven itself, wonderful as heaven itself was. The greatest wonder that John saw in heaven was, in his own words, a man-child, with whom a woman had travailed in birth, and who had now been caught up unto God and to the throne of God. John had been greatly favoured. Greatly favoured! For he had seen the two extremes—so to call them—of his master's life. And these are some of those extremes that John had in his mind, and in his heart, as he stood and looked at that great wonder. The one extreme was this. "And she brought forth her firstborn Son, and wrapped Him in swaddling clothes, and laid Him in a manger, because there was no room for them in the inn. The foxes have holes, and the birds of the air have nests, but the Son of Man hath not where to lay His head. Now, in the morning, as He returned into the city, he hungered." And then, the Garden of Gethsemane; and then, His arrest and His trial; and then, His crucifixion.

And now, there is the other extreme! "He humbled Himself, and became obedient unto death, even the death of the Cross. Wherefore

God hath highly exalted Him and hath given Him a name which is above every name, that, at the name of Jesus, every knee should bow, of things in heaven, and things in earth, and things under the earth: and that every tongue should confess that Jesus Christ is Lord, to the glory of God the Father." Our hearts are surely made of stone, since we can be told all that, without one thrill either of wonder or of worship. But the day is at the door, when he will have His revenge on us for all our indifference towards Him, and all our unbelief about Him. A day when every knee shall bow, and when we shall all fall at His feet as dead. These dark scales that are sealed down so close on our eyes today shall fall off every eye on that day. And every eye shall see Him, and shall see nothing else.

> The bride eyes not her garment,
>   But her dear bridegroom's face;
> I will not gaze at glory,
>   But on my King of grace—
> Not at the crown He gifteth,
>   But at His pierced hand:
> The Lamb is all the glory
>   Of Immanuel's land.

"If I could but look at Him through the keyhole of heaven, I would be satisfied," says Samuel Rutherford in his own intoxicated and enraptured way.

3. But, to me, there will be a far greater "wonder" in heaven than the whole of heaven itself. Ay, a far greater wonder than that glorified Manchild Himself. For, after all, heaven is His Father's house, and His own proper home and inheritance. But when I awake, and find myself in heaven—*that* will swallow up all heaven's other wonders to me. Is this, in very deed, myself? Am I actually, and in reality, in heaven? Am I made meet, at last, for the inheritance of the saints in light? Am I, O my God, at last set free from sin? Am I now to be for ever delivered from that hell-born thing that poisoned every hour of my life on the earth, and that so blasted, to me, the best joys of earth? O, saints and angels of God, say to me and assure me, that I am not in a dream! Confirm me, O ye holy ones, that I am not beside myself! Come, all ye shining hosts of His, and see as you pass by on

your errands of glory—come and see if, in all your seven heavens, there is another wonder of redeeming love, and saving grace, like me!

These, then, will be the first three, as I think, of the great wonders that we shall see in heaven. Heaven itself; Jesus Christ, the Son of Man, risen from the dead, ascended, exalted, and glorified; and, far above all, myself—so every saved sinner will say—every saved sinner, that is, who has one spark of self-knowledge, and one atom of a truly thankful heart.

4. And then, when once we have time to walk about Zion, to tell the towers thereof, to mark her bulwarks, and to consider her palaces; and when the ministering spirits shall join themselves to us, and shall say to us, "See what manner of stones and what buildings are here!"—we shall answer them that we have come out to this gate of God to see a sight that they cannot see, and to reflect upon a matter that they cannot comprehend. For, verily, "He took not on Him the nature of angels, but He took on Him the seed of Abraham." And they will wonder at us, and at what it is that we are seeing, as we so long continue to look down at the hole of the pit out of which we were digged, and at the hole of the rock whence we were hewn. At the hole of the pit, and then at the way, there it all is as clear as daylight now: all the way He has led and carried us, till our feet stand within thy gates, O Jerusalem! "And thou shalt remember all the way which the Lord thy God led thee these forty years in the wilderness, to humble thee, and to prove thee, and to know what was in thine heart. Thou shalt also consider in thine heart that as a man chasteneth his son, so the Lord thy God chasteneth thee." William Cowper counted himself the greatest wonder in all England. "I am surely the only convert in all England that was ever made in a madhouse," he said. Perhaps so. But, Bedlam and all—to borrow Cowper's own strong word—there will be saved sinners standing beside Cowper on that day, and at that earth-commanding gate, who will put both him and his blood-bought harp to silence with a conversion, and with an after lifetime of God's forbearance and long-suffering—far, far more wonderful than his.

5. And then, when at another time we stand on the sea of glass, and look down into its transparent depths—what a wonderful revelation that will be! We sang about it this morning. But we have

forgotten already what we sang about it. For, we sang it like men not yet awaked from their sleep, so little was the wonder and the worship: so little was the faith and the love with which we sang it. We sang these wonderful words:

> Thy mercy, Lord, is in the heavens:
> Thy truth doth reach the clouds:
> Thy justice is like mountains great;
> Thy judgments deep as floods.

And we read, and, shame to us to say, wholly without emotion, such a magnificent passage as this: "O the depth of the riches, both of the wisdom and the knowledge of God! How unsearchable are His judgments, and His ways past finding out!" But we shall awaken, once we are in heaven. For, once we are there, our eyes will receive such an unction that they will see down into those deep ways of God that were far past our finding out on earth. For His ways with us on earth are "as high as heaven, what can we do? They are deeper than hell, what can we know?" But we shall all find out the Almighty to perfection in heaven. "There is a path that no fowl knoweth, and which the vulture's eye hath not seen. The lion's whelps have not trod it, nor the fierce lion passed by it." And that unfathomable path is none other than that wonderful way, both of providence and of grace, on which He leads all His people home from earth to heaven, and from grace to glory. When a pastor is out among his sorely afflicted people, he is oftentimes struck absolutely dumb before the depth and the darkness of God's judgments. There are times and places where he cannot open his mouth, so dark and so full of distress are God's ways with this and that soul. He has neither the experience, nor the faith, nor the hope, that he would need to have, who would venture out as a comforter to those who are going up through such a great tribulation. God's ways are sometimes so absolutely overwhelming that it sounds cruel and heartless to go and repeat promises that are never to be fulfilled in this world.

But the boldest promises in all the believer's Bible will all be fulfilled in heaven, the postponed answers to all the promises will be heaped up, and made to run over in heaven. And those elect saints, whose lives of such suffering were the stumbling-stone of their boldest comforters, will there be found to God's incomparable and everlasting praise. Till that terrible sufferer, who spent all his days in a furnace seven times heated, will come forth without a hair of his head singed, or so much as the smell of the furnace fire upon his garments; and his song, among all the songs of the glorified, will for ever be: "O the depth! O the depth! O the depth of the wisdom, and the knowledge, and the grace of God to me!"

6. And then, while all these wonders, and all these new songs, are surrounding the gates of heaven, and are covering the shores of the sea of glass, the Word Himself will choose a select discipleship of the most seraphic intelligences from among the glorified, and will lead them up into the council-chamber of the past eternity. And in that great chamber there will be disclosed the secret wheels—wheel within his wheel—as if a wheel were in the midst of a wheel: all the living wheels—first of predestination, and then of providence, and then of grace, and then of glory, and every living wheel full of eyes within and without. And all these mystical wheels working together with such silence, with such speed, and with such sureness; and all fulfilling, to perfection, the will and the wisdom, and the everlasting love of Almighty God:

> Deep in unfathomable mines
>   Of never-failing skill,
> He treasures up His bright designs
>   And works His sovereign will.
> Blind unbelief is sure to err
>   And scan His work in vain:
> He is His own interpreter,
>   And He will make it plain.

7. And to complete and crown all, there will be the fulfillment of this fine promise, "In my Father's house are many mansions: I go to prepare a place for you." And it will be so. For you will all find a place prepared for yourselves in heaven. "When I awake, I shall be satisfied," said the psalmist, and so will you. For one thing—all the affections of your hearts will find their full outlet, their full delight, and their full fruition, there.

All your talents also will be multiplied, and perfected, and occupied there. Intellectual men are unwilling to become old and die; they so enjoy the occupations and the operations of their minds; they so delight in the search for truth, and in its discovery, that they hate the approach of old age, and the very name of death and the grave. But not believing, not heavenly-minded men. You will see them still learning new languages at threescore and ten. You will see their minds still opening to new truth at fourscore and ten. And they are wise and right, those probationers of immortality. For their "death," as we unbelievers so heathenishly call it, is not death to them. Death does not come near them. You cannot put them into your open graves. Death does not even seriously suspend their studies. "Today," says the wisdom of God to them, "you shall be with Me where there is no more night: and where there is no darkness at all. Today I shall, Myself, meet you, and introduce you to serve My Father day and night in His temple of truth, and love, and all the fullness of everlasting life." What a wonderful world we are in, my brethren! And what a wonderful world awaits us! Especially, and supremely, all you who are men of a sanctified mind. For all your best books, all your best apparatus, all your best instruments, all your suspended experiments on nature and on grace, all your hindered and all your interrupted enterprises, with all your gained and garnered knowledge—when you awake, you will find it all waiting you there as the reward of your high industry and your noble diligence here. "Well done, good and faithful servant! Enter thou on new worlds of truth, and knowledge, and love never to be exhausted, and never to be arrested or defeated."

In our ignorance and irreverence, we charge God foolishly as often as a young theologian, or a young scholar, or a young preacher, or a young man of science, is summoned up out of our sight. But if we were wise, and if we loved them, we would rejoice for their sake, even when we weep inconsolably for our own lifelong desolation. "For the throne of God and of the Lamb shall be in it: and His servants shall serve Him. And they shall see His face, and His name shall be in their foreheads. And they need no candle, neither light of the sun: for the Lord God giveth them light, and they shall reign for ever and ever."

When William Cowper died, there came out upon his sad countenance a look of "holy surprise." The very last poem Cowper had composed was about himself, and he had entitled it "The Castaway." But, instead of being what he thought he would for ever be, a look of "holy surprise" came out of his heart, and spread over his dead face—so abundant was the entrance that was being at that moment administered to him.

Come then, away, O downcast soul! Come away! And William Cowper, and you, and I, will one day hold a three-cornered contest in heaven as to which of us three has the most wonderful story to tell, and the most wonderful song to sing. I think I know who will carry away the prize from you both.

Nay, I am sure I know! "Of whom I am chief."

PART TWO
Mercy and Truth Are Met Together

8

The Locust-Eaten Past

A New Year Message

That which the palmerworm hath left hath the locust eaten; and that which the locust hath left hath the cankerworm eaten; and that which the cankerworm hath left hath the caterpillar eaten (Joel 1:4).
I will restore to you the years that the locust hath eaten (Joel 2:25).

Dr. Pusey, the most literal, orthodox, and conservative of commentators, admits, in his great work on the minor prophets, that the prophet Joel opens his book with an enigma. The locust and the palmerworm and the caterpillar and the cankerworm, he is compelled to admit, are clearly some sort of sacred enigma. That extraordinarily learned and extraordinarily painstaking interpreter absolutely ransacks all the books of natural history and of Eastern travel determined to find Joel's literal locusts in some of those books. But without success. For, terrible as are the tales that travellers tell about the locust, harrowing as are the accounts they give of the doomed lands on which the locust descends—after all that, there are some things in Joel still more terrible and still more harrowing. In his determination to find actual locusts, and nothing but actual locusts on the inspired page, the aged and saintly scholar toils on until, at last, he is compelled to lay down his books both of science and of travel, and to confess that he is beaten. "No," he says, "it is clear to me now that they are not literal locusts. Whatever they are they are not literal locusts. There is something here, I see now, far worse than any locust. There is some dark riddle of human misery here that neither our learned naturalists nor our Eastern travellers know everything about. But I think I know now," says the ripe old saint. "Joel's locusts,

I see now and am sure, are not so far away as Arabia or Palestine. For all Joel's locusts, in all their kinds and in all their devastations, are in my own heart. Why did I go beating about among blind and barren books when this prophet, all the time, was but describing the sinfulness of my own heart?" Dr. Pusey went far wrong and he led his church far wrong on some most essential matters, but he never went far wrong in his doctrines of sin and of holiness. And he was wholly right—as wholly right as the Holy Ghost and a holy life could make him—in his final and full explanation of this prophet's terrible locusts. "Let my readers take my word for it," he said. All this power and passion and repentance and remorse comes from a far deeper source than any plague of locusts. No! This is no locust. This is no deadly insect with shining wings. There is only one thing on the face of the whole earth that this can be. *This is sin!*

The first thing that aroused the great scholar's suspicion that the prophet was setting a deep riddle to his readers was this terrible passage: "Hear this, ye old men, and give ear, all ye inhabitants of the land. Tell your children of it, and let your children tell their children, and their children another generation. That which the palmerworm hath left hath the locust eaten; and that which the locust hath left the cankerworm hath eaten; and that which the cankerworm hath left hath the caterpillar eaten." In all his immense apparatus of authors the old Hebrew professor could find no breed of locust that ever came up, scourge after scourge, on any land, in that fashion. As far as he could read or hear, one descent of locusts is enough to make any land a desert. No. It clearly cannot be literal locusts. It is some deep riddle of desolation that the sorrowful prophet sets to us under the name of locusts.

And no sooner had the saintly scholar tried the key of sin than the prophet's sacred lock flew open, and his deep riddle was as clear as day. Try that key yourselves, my brethren. You have a great scholar's word for it that that key fits, to perfection, the most inward and intricate parts of Joel's inward and intricate prophecy. Well—try that same key upon yourselves. Try it on your own desolate life. Try it on desolation after desolation of your utterly desolate life. Try it year after year. Take sin after sin, sin after sin, and see if sin is not the true key of your desolate life.

The old men are challenged by this bold prophet to testify to the truth of what he says, to give their children and their children's children the benefit of their desolate and accumulated experience. Will you who are old men and wise do it? You are not great pulpit expositors like Gregory, nor great scholars like Pusey; but by this time you must be as wise and well-experienced as any ancient or modern of them all in the things that turn the garden of youth into the wilderness of old age. If you have learned anything to be called learning, you must have surely learned this—how one sin succeeds another till you are what you are today. You could name to your children—as Joel challenged the old men of his day to name to their children—you could name your locust-sins in their genealogical order, in their successive descents, and in their complete desolation. Name them then, first to yourselves and then to your children; and it will be your salvation and theirs.

But all this time, locusts—let us be thankful—do not descend on our land like that. Our cold, hard, dark, uncongenial climate has its compensations. If our fields are not so full of milk and honey and wine and oil as the Land of Judah is, neither have we those terrible scourges that the prophet here handles with such terrible power. It is only the richest and sunniest lands that breed locusts; and it is not your dark, cold, hard, uncongenial hearts that suffer from an inward sinfulness that makes life to some men such a wilderness. Some men will not understand this, and will not have it. But there are other men to whom this will read as the most literal, and so to say, scientific truth—*this* out of this prophet's so marvellously constructed riddle. "The land is as the Garden of Eden before them, and behind them a desolate wilderness: yea, and nothing shall escape them. Before their face the people shall be much pained, and all faces shall gather blackness. They shall run like mighty men; they shall climb the wall like men of war; and they shall march everyone on his ways, and they shall not break their ranks. They shall run to and fro in the city; they shall run upon the wall; they shall climb up upon the houses; they shall enter in at the windows like a thief. And, because of them, is not our meat cut off before our eyes? Yea, is not joy and gladness cut off from the house of our God? The seed is rotten under the clod because of them. The garner is desolate. And the barns are broken down." Oh! It is so true! So true, and so masterly that for the moment we forget our anguish in our sheer intellectual delight in it. That is prophecy! That is preaching! And there is a certain noble if bitter pleasure in seeing ourselves and our great enemy so divinely discovered, understood, and described. With such truth and power and passion and splendid eloquence is the multitudinousness, and the veracity, and the prolificness, and the ineradicableness of our sinfulness set forth in this prophet's tremendous pages.

But the word of the Lord came again to Joel the son of Pethuel. "Therefore, thus saith the Lord, turn ye even to Me with all your heart, and with fasting, and with weeping, and with mourning. And rend your heart, and not your garments, and turn unto the Lord. For He is gracious and merciful, and repenteth Him of the evil." "Rend your heart!" prophesied the son of Pethuel with all his power. "And so we shall," replied the old men of his day. "So we shall; and so we have already done!" said many of the inhabitants of the locust-cursed land. "If a 'rent heart' is to be the arrest of God's judgments, and the return of His mercies, then let Him look and see if our hearts are not truly rent," witnessed the worshippers in Zion. "Let Him search us and try us," they said, "if our hearts are not enough rent. Rend our hearts, O Lord!" They proclaimed a fast and prayed. And so you do also, who are old men and wise men, and elders in Zion. "If we know ourselves," you say, "our hearts are indeed rent before God. We have nothing to offer to God or man out of the fields of our past lives, but a rent heart. That is the only redress or reparation and recompense we can offer to God or man. Blessed be God that a rent heart is His best harvest!" you exclaim.

"Who knoweth?" wonders the prophet—"who knoweth if He will return and repent, and leave a blessing behind Him?" And that both His prophet and His people might know, and might not be left in any doubt, the word of the Lord came again: "Fear not, but be glad and rejoice; for the Lord will do great things. I will do even this great thing, saith the Lord. I will restore to you the years that the locust hath eaten." Now, all parable apart, and in all plainness of speech, can any one tell us in what way the God of Israel, and our own God, does that? Set the locusts aside for a little, and tell us in plain words that we can understand and remember, just how our past years can be recovered and restored; or, if that is impossible, then just what God can do and will do for us, if our heart is rent and laid at His feet.

Well, for one thing, Joel and his old men had reaped the fruit of a "rent heart." A harvest that we have reaped also, have we not, my brethren? Our hearts, like Joel's, have a rent in them so deep, so wide, so ragged, that nothing in this world, not all the milk and wine and honey of this world, will ever heal it. We have brought a heart out of our past years that no future years on earth can ever again make what it once was. We would not have it again what it once was, even if we could. For our heart is now rent loose from earth at its best, and gone on beforehand to heaven. It will not be healed and made whole and satisfied short of "His likeness." What fruit? Well—a "rent heart" to begin with; and with a "rent heart," a humbled heart, a heart full of humility, and self abasement, and self-abhorrence, and self-abandonment. And a mind to dwell beside such a heart, and to minister to it—even a spiritual and a heavenly mind. A mind and a heart for spiritual things: that is to say, for the things of God in nature, and in His Word, and in Jesus Christ, and in grace, and in glory. A heart and a mind for the cross of Christ, and for the throne of grace, and for the hopes and foretastes of everlasting life.

But Paul answers his own questions best. For these are his own noble words—that "godly sorrow for the past worketh repentance for the future not to be repented of. For, behold, this selfsame thing, what carefulness it wrought in you! Yea, what clearing of yourselves. Yea, what indignation; yea, what fear; yea, what vehement desire. Yea, what zeal; yea, what revenge." Or take it in Andrewes' fine paraphrase: "Turn, O Lord, my mourning into dancing; my dreaming into earnestness; my many falls into so many clearings of myself; my guilt into indignation: my sin into fear; my transgression into vehement desire; my unrighteousness into zeal; and my pollution into revenge." Or, again, let Fenelon reply to Paul. "I downright rejoice in your desolation," he writes to a noble lady correspondent. "For God will teach you how to kill self out of your heart through disgust at this world, and through the desolation of your own life. As to grave faults of your past life they will turn to your certain good in the future if you make use of them for your humiliation. The true way to profit out of an evil past is to face it in all its hideousness, hoping for nothing better from ourselves in the time to come, while, at the same time, we do not cease to hope in God. And when He has stripped us bare of all strength and hope and self-resource, He will then begin to graft us on upon His Son Jesus Christ." That, in the plainest possible words, is some of the fruit we have ever with us, out of those years of which we are now ashamed. Those are some of the ways in which God restores to his people the years that the cankerworm hath eaten.

It has been the want of faith, my brethren, that has been at the root of all the blight and barrenness of our past years. And if God is to make His promise in the text good to you and me for this New Year, and for all our own future years, it will be strengthening and fertilising our faith! When the root is weak or diseased, or when it has no deepness of earth, then any passing locust will soon kill the tree. But when the root is sound and strong and deep-seated and well-watered, the tree will blossom and bear fruit and will survive all the locusts that you can send up against it. Let us have faith, then, my brethren. Let us have, and in all things let us exercise, faith in God. Let us believe that He is, as we have never up to this year believed. Let us believe His Word. Let us read and meditate on His Word in a way we have never yet done. Our spiritual life and its fruitfulness comes and goes just as we read God's Word, and meditate on it in secret. Let us read, then, and meditate, read and pray, till His Word dwells in us richly. And then, faith and all its fruits will grow in us, as they have always grown in those who had the true root within them, and who watered it with the water of life that flows in the channels of God's Word. And then, with the life of faith growing in that way in us—what new creatures we shall soon become! What new eyes will begin to open in our hearts! And what a new world on earth and in heaven our new eyes will begin to see! And what years, even on earth, we shall yet have, as faith puts forth in us her perfect fruit! Believe! Believe! Have faith! Have faith!—our Lord went about continually pleading with men. And when He found faith, in Jew or Gentile, how proud He was of it! What liberty and boldness He allowed it! And what rewards He put upon it!

And with a faith like that for the root of our future life, a holy love will henceforth be the sap, and strength, and the fatness of our redeemed and remaining years. O, if God would but shed abroad His love in our hearts, we should soon forget all the famine and desolation of our past years! And He will! He says that He will, and we believe Him. Do we not, do you not, in these days feel something begun and going on within you as if a new beginning of faith and love was come to you? Do you not feel something, not unlike the breath of a spiritual spring, beginning to blow over your long desolation? I do. Do you not? O, let us all set open our hearts to the Spirit of God, and the buds will soon begin to burst and the birds will soon begin to build and to sing. Open your hearts to God, my brethren! Do not be afraid of God. Where are you going? To whom can you go if you go away from God? God is love. If God is anything, He is love. God is also light in darkness, and warmth in winter, and companionship and communion in desertion and loneliness, and goodness, and truth, and beauty, and sweetness, and more than mortal tongue can tell. It is well worth being the chief of sinners to have such a Saviour. It is well worth having all our years within us eaten up of locusts to have a message that God sent us all this morning. And this message, as the Lord liveth, is no lie, but is the simple truth. It is no dream. It is no delusion. It is the surest, solidest, most matter-of-fact, most verifiable, most experimental, most immediate, most urgent, and most everlasting of all truths. Heaven and earth shall pass away. You will be present and will see and feel them passing away—but this message of this morning shall not pass till it is all fulfilled. Rend your hearts, and who knoweth what He will do? Turn to the Lord and see. Gather up your lost life, and lay it down at His feet, and see. Say to Him that you have destroyed yourself, and see. Say to Him that all your hope is in His Word, and see. And then, tell ye your children what He hath done for your soul, and let your children tell their children, and their children to another generation.

Be ye glad, then, ye children of Zion; and rejoice in the Lord your God. For I will restore to you the years that the locust hath eaten, and the cankerworm, and the caterpillar and the palmerworm. And ye shall eat in plenty, and be satisfied and praise the name of the Lord your God that hath dealt so wondrously with you. And ye shall know that I am in the midst of my people Israel: and My people shall never be ashamed.

9

What Think Ye of Christ?

What think ye of Christ? (Matt. 22:42).

What think ye of Christ? That is the question of all questions. No other question so important and so pressing as that question has ever been put to the mind, and to the heart, and to the conscience of man. There is no other possible question that so taxes and so tests the whole soul of every man as just this question—what he thinks of Christ. This question is "quick, and powerful, and sharper than any two-edged sword, piercing even to the dividing asunder of soul and spirit, and of the joints and marrow, and is a discerner of the thoughts and intents" of every human heart. What, then, think ye of Christ?

1. But to begin with—and by far the most important question of all—what does God think of Christ? Well, the whole Bible is full of little else but of what God thinks of Christ. As thus: "Behold, My Servant, Whom I uphold: Mine elect, in Whom My soul delighteth. A bruised reed shall He not break, and the smoking flax shall He not quench. Therefore will I divide Him a portion with the great, and He shall divide the spoil with the strong."

And then, when Christ actually came, and when He was being baptized into His work, lo, a voice from heaven, saying, "This is My Beloved Son, in Whom I am well pleased." And when His great work was for ever finished, we have this: "Wherefore God hath highly exalted Him, and hath given Him a Name which is above every name, that at the Name of Jesus every knee should bow." Such are some samples of God's thoughts and declarations concerning His Son, Jesus Christ our Lord.

2. And then, next in importance to what God thinks of Christ, what does Christ think of Himself? My brethren—what a mystery the young Christ must have been for long years to Himself! I suppose "He began to be about thirty years of age," before He was at all able to satisfy Himself as to Who and What He actually was. The Holy Child Jesus must have made the discovery early in His life that he was like no other child in all Israel. "All seek their own," says Holy Scripture, in condemnation of all the children of men. But the Child Jesus must have seen and felt within Himself, with a holy wonder, and holy joy, that, while all around Him, young and old were all seeking their own things, far deeper in His heart than His own things were the things of God, and the things of His neighbour. So early was this the case with Him that, at twelve years of age, He was able to say to His mother: "How is it that ye sought me? Wist ye not that I must be about My Father's business?" And then, after another eighteen years' incessant observation, examination, and study of Himself, with much searching of the Scriptures, and with much prayer, He was enabled to come forth from His obscurity, and to announce Himself and to offer Himself to Israel, as her promised Messiah, and to all men as their promised Redeemer.

3. Now, after all that, what an additional study and what a splendid study it would make to go on to ask and to answer what the Apostle John thought of Christ—John, who lay in his Master's bosom, and enjoyed His Master's special confidence and His special love. And what Peter ultimately thought of Him Whom at one time he had denied with oaths and curses. And what Judas Iscariot thought of his master all along—and at the end. It would throw a flood of light, both upon the traitor himself, and upon his whole time, if we could only get at his real thoughts about Christ. But above all—what Paul thought, Paul in whom "God revealed His Son," as never before, nor since. And then, what the Greek and Latin Fathers—those so deep and so clear thinkers—thought, in their day, of Christ. And then, the Reformers—Luther and Calvin and Knox, and all that profound and spiritual school—what they thought of the greatest subject of thought to men and angels. And then, what the English Puritans

What Think Ye of Christ?

taught the English people and the American people to think of Christ. And then, our own Scottish forefathers, with the enthralled and enraptured Rutherford at their head—what they all thought and spoke to their people concerning Christ. To tell all that in detail would be of the first interest and the first importance. But after all, this would remain *the real question*—What think we of Christ? You sitting there and I standing here.

4. Now, in this congregation, as in every congregation, there must be various ranks and classes of people who divide themselves out before God just according as they think of Christ. For, "as a man thinketh in his heart, so is he." Our Lord once said of Himself that His coming among men had brought not peace, but a sword. And not a sword only, but a broad and a deep dividing line also. Many dividing lines, indeed; many clefts indeed, and chasms even; many all-but-impassable gulfs, already open between man and man among us, according as we think of Christ. One sad, and not small class among us, is composed of those men and women who simply never think of Christ at all. They are exactly like John Bunyan: they never think, in church or market, whether there is a Christ or no.

But happily, there is another class of men and women among us who are the exact opposite of that. They are but a small class, it is to be feared, in any congregation, and yet, who can tell? They may be more in number than any one would believe. Few or many, this noble class is composed of those men and women among us who in their heart of hearts are continually thinking of Christ. "To me to live is Christ," says Paul. "What things were gain to me, those I counted loss for Christ," he says again. "Christ Jesus," he says in another place, "is made of God to me wisdom, and righteousness, and sanctification, and redemption." And so on: through all his Epistles, so full of Christ, and of nothing else but Christ. Now, they cannot be a great crowd in any congregation or community, who say such things as these concerning Christ. But there are such men and women among us: "one of a city and two of a family," as the prophet says. Yes, we will believe it: there are truly Christian men and women among us, and more than you would easily believe, who say to Christ with all their heart every returning morning: "When I awake I am still with Thee!"

> Dark and cheerless is the morn
> Unaccompanied by Thee.
> Joyless is the day's return
> Till Thy mercy's beams I see.

But, with all their happy experiences of Christ, even the best of believers too much forget to think of Him when they are suddenly surprised with some unforeseen temptation, or heavy trial, or sharp cross, or sore hurt, or great loss. But the root of the matter is in them all the time. And they soon recover their feet, and say to Christ: "Whom have I, and whom need I, but Thee alone?" The very best of believers will have seasons of the most terrible depression, and desolation, and despair. But the sun shines out, and they are themselves again. That is to say—Christ is Himself to them again. Ups and downs like these go on with the best of believers, all through their life on earth. Till "the souls of all true believers are at their death made perfect in holiness, and do immediately pass into glory." That is to say, into the glory of Christ: according to His all-prevailing prayer in their behalf—"Father, I will that they also whom Thou hast given Me be with Me where I am."

And then, besides those among us who never think of Christ at all, and those who think of little else, there is a large, intermediate class, to whom this great matter may be put in some such way as this. Let me put it to you in this way, this morning: Suppose it were discovered to you that there is no Christ, that there has never been a Christ, and never will be, and that the whole thing is a delusion. Suppose that you were able to send out trusty spies, to search both earth and heaven, to their utmost borders. And suppose your spies came back and reported to you that they had done what you instructed them to do: that they had explored the whole universe, in the height and in the depth, and had found no Christ, nor any one at all to answer in any respect to the New Testament description of Christ— What would you think? What would you say? What would you do? Would that report be a great relief to you? Would you breathe far more freely after that? What would you give to your spies for their reward? And how would you find words to thank them? Would you tell them what an unspeakable service they had done you? Would you confess to them how unhappy the thought of ever having to meet with Christ face to face had always made you? Would you shake hands with them, and say: Come and dine with me. Come and let us eat meat and drink wine and be merry, since there is no Christ, and no judgment seat of Christ, and no book to be opened, and no account to be given to Him of the deeds we have done in our body? Is anything like that your true state of mind concerning Christ? Or, on the other hand, would you say to the spies who reported that there is no Christ, that they had made you of all men most miserable? Would your first words be to curse the day on which you were born? Would your face, from that day, more and more gather blackness? Would you be like Elijah, who went a day's journey into the wilderness, and came and sat down under a juniper tree and requested for himself that he might now die, and said, "It is enough. Now, O God, take away my life"?

By putting the thing to ourselves in some such ways as these, we are better able to read the deepest and secretest thoughts of our hearts about Christ and about ourselves. And indeed, any device is admissible, and is wise, that arouses us to think at all about Christ, and whether there is a Christ, or no.

But, whatever your spies say to you about Christ—whether they bring back a false report like the ten, or a true report like Caleb and Joshua; whether they tell you their abominable lies about Christ, or tell you the divine truth about Him—be that as it may; at any rate, no man can tell you lies about yourself. You know yourself better than any other man can possibly know you. What, then, do you think and say of yourself? That is, to you, the first and foremost of all questions. That comes even before what you think of Christ. For it is what you think of yourself that will always decide what you think of Him. Tell me what you think of yourself, and I will undertake to tell you what and how much you think of Christ. Just as, tell me what and how much and how often you think of Christ, and I will already know how to a certainty what you think of yourself. The plain truth is: no one but a convinced sinner can think one right thought about Jesus Christ. And more than that, the greater the sinner, the greater and truer will his thoughts be about his Saviour. Jesus Christ, the

Son of God, is ten thousand things to God, and man, and angel: ten thousand things on earth and in heaven, in time and in eternity, in grace and in glory; but, first and foremost, to you and to me this morning, He is our Saviour from our sins. Select real sinners, then, for your spies, if you would have a true report concerning Christ, and whether there is a Christ or no. Select and send the very chief of sinners if you would have the whole truth told you about Christ. Ask them to search and to report to you, and say to them when they return: "Saw ye Him whom my soul loveth?" And they will tell you that they found both heaven and earth as full as they can hold of Christ and of no one else but Christ. And that He sent this message by them to you: "Come unto Me, all ye that labour, and are heavy laden. And him that cometh to Me I will in no wise cast out." And then, when you go to Him, and are not cast out, come back and tell us about Him. Tell us what you found Him to be, and what you now think of Him. And then, after that, you shall always be our spies; you shall always be our Caleb and our Joshua; and we will reward you, and your children, with a south land, and with springs of water, because you brought us a true and encouraging and a cheering report concerning Christ, your Saviour and ours.

Now, in closing, let us go over and tell to ourselves, and to one another, some of the things that have helped us most to our best thoughts concerning Christ. There are so many things in this world that work the other way; there are so many things that cause us to forget Christ, that it is wise and good to go over, and keep well in mind, the things that have best assisted us in our best thoughts concerning Christ. Well, then, what is it in Christ that you most admire? What is it in Him that most moves your heart? What is it in Him that makes your heart sing within you and to say: "Thou art fairer than the children of men"? To what incident in His recorded life on earth do you like best to return? What miracle of His do you always ask to be repeated in you? What mighty work of His do you pray importunately to have worked over again in your son or in your daughter? What sermon of His do you oftenest return to hear? What parable of His do you esteem to be His gem and His masterpiece? What secret prayer of yours has He so openly and so wonderfully answered? What blessing do you possess at this moment that you got from Him when you asked Him for it? Or, perhaps you got it before you had even so much as asked Him for it! By what name of His do you oftenest call upon Him in prayer or in praise? Do you say:

> Jesus, my Shepherd, Husband, Friend,
>   My Prophet, Priest, and King,
> My Lord, my Life, my Way, my End,
>   Accept the praise I bring?

What name of His will be most legibly written on your forehead in heaven, to be read there by saints and angels?

"Can you tell us," said Prudence, "by what means you find your thoughts most turned to Christ?"

"Yes," Christian said, "when I think what I saw at the Cross, that will do it. And when I look on my broidered coat, that will do it. Also, when I look into the roll that I carry in my bosom, that will do it. And when my heart waxes warm about whither I am going, that will do it."

"And what is it that makes you so desirous to go to Mount Zion?" she went on to ask.

"Why, there I hope to see Him alive that did hang dead upon the Cross for me. And there I hope to be rid of all those things that are to this day such a grief and such a snare to me. And there I shall dwell with the company I like best. For, to tell you the truth, I love Him because I was by Him relieved of my burden, and I am weary of this inward sickness of mine. And I would fain be where I shall sin no more, and with that company that shall continually cry: Holy! Holy! Holy!"

"When Jesus came into the coasts of Caesarea Philippi, He asked His disciples, saying, Whom do men say that I, the Son of Man, am? … Some say that Thou art John the Baptist; some Elias; and others, Jeremias or one of the prophets … But whom say ye that I am? And Simon Peter answered and said, Thou art the Christ, the Son of the living God.

"And Jesus answered and said unto him: Blessed art thou, Simon Bar-Jona: for flesh and blood hath not revealed it unto thee, but My Father which is in heaven."

10

The Corn of Wheat

...Jesus answered them, saying, The hour is come, that the Son of Man should be glorified. Verily, verily, I say unto you: except a corn of wheat fall into the ground and die, it abideth alone: but if it die, it bringeth forth much fruit...
(John 12:20–33).

The Greek people, if so be they were our Greeks, had gifts given them by God above all people that ever dwelt on the face of the earth. Above all other people they had the seeing eye, and the hearing ear, the love of all beauty, and the desire after all wisdom. Art, song, eloquence, letters, philosophy: what had the Greek people not? Let our Lord and His great Apostles answer. They had not salvation: "Salvation is of the Jews," said our Lord. With all their wisdom, they knew not God, said the Apostle writing to the Corinthians. That is to say, they knew not the law of God; they knew not sin; and therefore they knew not salvation. And thus it is that we find in the text certain Greeks who have come up to worship at Jerusalem, and to take part in its Passover. "The same came therefore to Philip, which was of Bethsaida of Galilee, and desired him, saying, Sir, we would see Jesus." A good errand and a welcome desire; only they had formed it and uttered it just a little too soon. For our Lord is still fulfilling, indeed, He is just finishing, the great mission on which He had been sent to "the lost sheep of the house of Israel." Had those Greeks waited, and come to Philip, say, six weeks after this, they would not indeed have "seen Jesus," but they would have heard, every man in his own tongue, the wonderful works of God. They would have found Peter preaching to this effect: "Repent, and be baptized every one of you in the name of Jesus Christ for the remission of sins. For the promise is unto you, and to your children and to all that are afar off, even as many as the Lord our God shall call."

But as it was, their visit to Philip and their message to Philip's Master were just a little premature. All things, though fast getting ready, were scarcely ready as yet. The middle wall of partition was not yet quite broken down. Those that were far off were not just yet to be made nigh. The enmity was not yet slain. The reconciliation of both Jew and Greek into one body was not yet fully accomplished. The One Spirit had not yet given both access unto the Father. In one word, Jesus Christ had not yet been crucified, much less glorified. And thus it is that we owe the priceless passage before us to this somewhat abrupt and premature petition of certain Greeks to see our Lord.

It is a proverb among us that though death may have been long looked for, yet, when it actually comes, it always comes suddenly. Death takes the best prepared men by surprise. And this too sudden message from those Greek proselytes took our Lord by surprise; for it brought Him too sharply, and too suddenly, face to face with His Cross. He had long been ready for it; He had long been labouring to make His disciples ready for it; but when the full *fruits* of it were thus suddenly demanded of Him, He reeled under the blow, and took some time to recover Himself. He felt that the cup was, at that moment, too suddenly thrust into His hand; and the Cross too suddenly laid upon His shoulders. "The hour has come then," He said, more to Himself than to any one else. And during that "hour," between the beginning of it and the end of it, He knew that He had to finish a work the bare thought of which at that moment threw Him back upon all the faith, all the filial obedience, all the strength and all the resolution that even *He* could command. He had been wont to set forth some of the things of the Kingdom of Heaven to His disciples in parables; and at that weak and over-weighted moment, He took up this powerful parable and laid it on His own heart to calm and subdue and strengthen it. It was far more to commit and confirm Himself at that heart-sinking moment than to instruct or console His disciples that He said in their hearing and presence: "Except a corn of wheat fall into the ground and die, it abideth alone: but if it die, it bringeth forth much fruit."

Just suppose it—they sometimes expected it: well, just suppose it—that our Lord had in anger and in judgment turned His back on rebellious Israel and had gone to the dispersed among the Gentiles. He might have been an accepted and an honoured teacher come from God among them; and He would thus have escaped the cross, and perhaps the hemlock cup also, and gone down to His grave in an honoured old age. *Suppose that,* I say: do violence to your feelings and your faith so far as for one moment to suppose that: the painful supposition, I do not say possibility, is involved in His own parable; then, in that case, *He* would have been the corn of wheat which abides alone. Had he done this, then in His own words—in loving His life He would have lost it. For He had not come to this world to live in this world, but to die in it and for it. He had come to Jerusalem and was now waiting in it to be offered up; and had He now flinched and fled—forgive the impossible thought—it is His own—*that* had been a fall of man worse far than the fall of fifty Adams. Let His redeemed pardon the impossible and dreadful dream; and let them boast themselves in their faithful and merciful Saviour, and say that it was by renouncing the offered office of a Greek sage at the end that He became the glorified Redeemer He now is, just as it was by refusing the offered throne of Solomon at the beginning that He now sits at the right hand of the throne of God.

But what is true of the parent seed that lies dead and buried in the fruitful furrow, that is true also in its turn of the full corn that is fast ripening in the autumn ear. Every single corn of springing wheat has the same sacrificial future standing before it. As soon as it becomes a ripe corn of wheat, this same parable is immediately prophesied over it. And not of wheat only, but much more of men is this parable true. "He that loveth His life shall lose it: while he that hateth his life in this world shall keep it unto life eternal." Look around you, my brethren, nay look within you and see if Jesus Christ is not in all this a true prophet. He among us who dies to his own life, he alone truly lives. He who lives and dies for others; he who works with his hands that he may have to give to him who needeth; he who stints his too-full table that he may deal his bread to the hungry; and gives up his own will and wish and way for peace and love and righteousness' sake—what is his reward? A prophet shall answer to him: "The Lord shall guide thee continually, and satisfy thy soul in drought, and make fat thy bones: and thou shalt be like a watered garden, and like a spring of water whose waters fail not." And still more true is it that he who loveth his own life shall lose it—for he has already lost it; he is already dead. He who spares himself and lives for himself; he who shuts up his hand and his heart from God and his neighbours—that man is already dead. He may be hoarding, or he may be feasting, as his humour is—as the nature of his corruption is—but he is already dead. They are already dead unto God—as many as live unto themselves. "Verily, verily, I say unto you, Except a corn of wheat fall into the ground and die, it abideth alone; but if it die it bringeth forth much fruit." Saw you ever a stalk of corn standing anywhere with its heavy head of edible gold? You did not need to dig up its hidden root in order to be sure that it had sprung up at first, and had been daily nourished out of the burst bosom and broken heart of a parent seed. When you next enter a wide harvest-field filled with rejoicing reapers, walk softly over it, for buried and forgotten beneath your feet there lies a great graveyard of parental seed. Buried around Bannockburn and Bothwell Brig lies the seed-corn of Scotland's civil and religious liberties. Is this a free New Testament Church? And is she the mother and sister of many such? Then, forget not, that she too purchased her own freedom and theirs at the great price set forth in the text: the price of forgotten generations of martyrs and confessors and outcast Fathers who counted not their lives dear to them, of whom the world was not worthy. The glorified Church herself will have this parable graven on her foundation-stone; this Scripture in gold around a cross in blood will be her legend and her mystery in the eyes of all her blood-redeemed and sorrow-sanctified members: "He that loveth his life shall lose it, but he that hateth his life shall keep it." Do I read aright? "He that *hateth his life.*" Did our Lord indeed say that? Did John understand his Master aright when he so reported Him? Or is this still the language of parable and paradox? No, my brethren, this is not in the parable at all; this is in the interpretation. Our Lord is here speaking plainly. Plainly, literally, prosaically: putting the right word, and the only right word, upon the thing. Yes, there is no doubt of it. Our Lord certainly said, "He that hateth his life." Now, do not be frightened or offended at this noble doctrine of deep hatred preached by Christ and practised to the letter by all His disciples. Do not be alarmed at their morose and misanthropical neighbourhood. Do not be too horrified at them: do not flee from them as if they were monsters. They will not bite you. They will not hurt a hair of your head. They will not even sit and speak against you. Not one ray of your reputation will be dimmed by them. Read the text again, "He that hateth his life," and so on. It is not his neighbour he hates. It is not his enemy. It is not even his more talented or more successful friend. It is himself—himself and his own sinful life. He has no hatred left for you; it is all poured out, poured in and expended on himself. Yes, my brethren, refine and distil till you get at the uttermost essence and the innermost affection of a man of God, true and safe for eternal life, and you will find that our Lord is not very far wrong when He says that the disciple who is likest his Master both in holy affections and in sacrificial fruits has his affections saturated, and their roots strengthened by the healing salt of true self-hatred. Away then with all your milk-and-water solutions and tame interpretations here! Take them to those who do not need and do not seek for and hunt for eternal life. Christ spoke to men and not to children, to manly saints and not eunuch-like sinners when He said, "He that hateth his life"! The author of *The Crook in the Lot* thus sums up his fifty-four years' experience of this hateful life: "Man is born crying, lives complaining, and dies disappointed. All is vanity and vexation of spirit. But I have waited for Thy salvation, O Lord." Wait so; wait with Him and you shall not be confounded and put to shame. For our Lord's interpretation of this parable thus concludes: "If any man serve Me, let him follow Me; and where I am, there shall also My servant be: if any man serve Me, him will My Father honour." But, the marvellous narrative proceeds: "Now is My soul troubled."

"Who is the Redeemer of God's elect" that He should so speak? "The only Redeemer of God's elect is the Lord Jesus Christ, Who, being the eternal Son of God, became man, and so was, and continueth to be, God and man in two distinct natures, and one Person for ever." Yes: "Two natures": "two distinct natures." Here in our text is one of the very best proofs of it. Our Lord, our Redeemer, was and is the Eternal Son of God, "the same in substance, equal in power and glory." But He "became man"; and He was and is as truly man as if He had not been God. Man, "made of a woman." Man, by "taking to Himself a true body and a reasonable soul." He speaks in the twenty-seventh verse: "Now is My soul troubled." Why, my brethren, here is a soul just like yours and mine! A soul troubled. A soul lifted up to heaven one moment, and cast down to the grave's mouth the next moment. Its Possessor preaching eternal life and glorification through the Cross with one breath—and with the next pouring out His soul in sighs and sobs, in prayers and supplications. After this do not upbraid your ministers too bitterly with the glaring inconsistency between their preaching and their practice. The disciple is not expected to be greater or better than his Master. Ah, my brethren, even to Jesus Christ, preaching was one thing and practice another. Rapture of soul in contemplation of heavenly truth and eternal life is one thing; and the upward path of the Cross is another. Those premature and obtrusive Greeks again smote against our Lord's heavy heart. For the moment He had almost forgotten their presence and their errand. For the moment He had been out of the body. But here again He sinks back into the body till He feels the thick darkness closing around it, and the nails and the spear crashing through it. The cup still stands before Him with the undrunk curse filling it. And again His "true body and His reasonable soul," His affectionate and passionate soul, shrank and trembled and were troubled.

It is out of instances like this that the Apostle generalises the heart-comforting character he gives to Christ as our great High Priest. "He was in all points tempted like as we are." For after all our earlier temptations have fallen off us, after our first fierce passions are all burnt to dross and dust under our feet, a new and more deadly access of temptations assails us: temptations to rebellion and bitterness against God and man, temptations to disappointment and disaffection, to envy and ill-will, to gloom and repining of soul, a settled stubbornness to accept and do and go through with the holy will of God. "Now is our soul troubled" at poverty; now at bereavement; now at bodily infirmity; now at some thorn in our flesh, or some crook in our lot; now at approaching age, and now at near and inevitable death. But then, so was our Lord. "Yet," blessed be His name, "without sin." Let all the afflicted people of God take this true comfort that it is only human nature to be troubled in soul under the pressure of temptation and affliction. And that it only becomes sin when affliction is nursed and brooded over and held close to an unbroken heart. Soul trouble only becomes sinful when prayer is restrained or forsaken; when the promises are treated lightly or set aside; and when the example and the grace of Christ are wilfully passed by and forgotten. Let it never be passed by or for one moment forgotten by any troubled soul that our Saviour was not and is not an oak or a rock, but was and is a Man of like passions and like affections with ourselves. And best of all, He has not to this day forgotten what He came through in the days of His soul trouble:

> He still remembers in the skies
> His tear, His agonies, and cries

And thus "His perturbations," as Augustine says "were for our tranquillity; and His infirmity for our fortification."

"Now is My soul troubled; and what shall I say?" I do not know what to say to express my thankfulness that this great Scripture has been preserved to us. I look on this as one of the most precious passages in all the afflicted man's Bible. "What shall I say?" cries out our Lord's staggered heart. He is in a sore strait. Duty is behind Him impelling Him on, while the Cross is before Him, terrifying Him back. God's law is in His heart; but the floods of fear and the horror of the death awaiting Him almost blot it out. What shall I say? He groans. Ah! Death! Death! Thou art indeed our last enemy! Thou puttest Standfast himself into a muse when thou presentest thy challenge! O my soul! after thou hast preached the resurrection of the dead for a lifetime, and comforted many sick-beds, and rebuked all unready and unwilling saints—how wilt thou thyself do in the swelling of Jordan? What wilt thou say when *thy* near death troubles *thee*?

Surely this:—"Father, glorify Thy name!" "Now is My soul troubled; and what shall I say? Father, save Me from this hour. Father, glorify Thy name; and I will pay the covenanted price." And now with that the bitterness of death is already past. The great trouble has passed off His soul, and communion with His Father is restored. And now, out of that sore but victorious experience, He returns to us and says to us: "If any man serve Me, let him follow Me; and where I am there shall also My servant be." My brethren, let us indeed follow such a master. Let nature cry out; let our hearts be never so much staggered and perplexed; let never so deep waters come over our head; let all God's waves and billows burst as they please upon us. Only at that awful hour let us follow Christ; let us call on Christ, and determine in His strength to imitate Him; and as He was so shall we immediately be in our trouble—faith and obedience shall win the victory.

And now, in His resignation and submission, in the consequent communion with His Father that follows this hour and power of darkness, our Lord looks up and faces without fear those ominous Greeks. He can now bear to look on them. He beams on them now and blesses them. He sees what Isaiah calls "His seed" flocking up behind them. Nay, who can tell but at that rapt and supreme moment He was shown some of ourselves, and saw from what His death would save some of us: till, from the sight and the thought, He drank in fresh strength and devotion and resolution till He was able to utter his great promise and prophecy—"I, if I be lifted up, will draw all men unto Me."

And, most mercifully to us, it has all come about, as that day He said it would. He has been so lifted up that He has drawn us. His Cross has become the true rendezvous and universal resort of the chief of sinners. The Desire of all nations was never found till Christ was crucified. But Christ crucified, like a Divine lodestone, has drawn to Calvary a multitude that no man can number of guilty and broken hearts. Calvary is the true centre and sanctuary of this fallen and broken world. The Cross, like a Divine keystone, holds its tottering and falling fabric together. By Christ and by His Cross "all things consist."

Hath He marks to lead me to Him
 If He be my Guide?
In His feet and hands are wound-prints,
 And His side!

Is there diadem, as Monarch,
 That His brow adorns?
Yea, a crown in very surety,
 But of thorns!

And it is as so lifted up, so stricken, so smitten of God, and so afflicted, that He ever draws me. It is as wounded for my transgressions and bruised for mine iniquities, and as so lifted up, that I can dare to come near to Him. But as so lifted up by the Father, His Father and my Father, He draws me to Him with all the intolerable burden of my sins and my sinfulness upon me. No one else so draws me. Not God, unless God in Christ; not man, unless the Man Christ Jesus. And no other Christ Jesus but the Christ Jesus of the Cross. No man knoweth or careth for my soul but this Man of my sorrows. All men else, when I come to them in my sin and misery, say to me, "See thou to that." But Jesus Christ and Him crucified, He draws me. As I come to Him with such confidence and such a confession, I am a wonder and an astonishment to myself. But still He draws me as often as Christ Crucified is preached unto me. Again, and even now, He draws me. As I speak of Him and hear of Him He again takes the millstone off my neck, opens my prison house, and pays my uttermost farthing. He takes off my fetters and puts a new song in my mouth. "O Lord," I am constrained to sing, "O Lord, truly I am Thy servant and the son of Thine handmaid. Thou hast loosed my bonds." And as I so come and so sing He hides me continually in the shadow of His cross as in a pavilion, shielding me, as I know very well, both from the righteous wrath of God and from the angry strife of men. "I draw all men unto Me." Yea, Lord, if Thou hast drawn me, and received me, and saved me—then all men may well yield to Thee, and trust in Thee, and abide in Thee.

"And I, if I be lifted up, will draw all Men unto Me. This He said, signifying what death He should die."

11

The Master and His Friends

Greater love hath no man than this, that a man lay down his life for his friends. Ye are My friends, if ye do whatsoever I command you. Henceforth I call you not servants; for the servant knoweth not what his lord doeth: but I have called you friends; for all things that I have heard of My Father I have made known unto you (John 15:13–15).

John has the supreme distinction, and the everlasting honour of having been our Lord's most intimate friend on earth. And what an exalted light that casts on the character of John, on the qualities of his mind, and on the disposition of his heart! Who are his friends? we ask when we would know all about a man. Who is his most intimate friend? we ask. No, do you ask that question about Zebedee's second son? Well, he was "the disciple whom Jesus loved." He was the one of the Twelve who leaned on his Master's bosom at the Last Supper. And he was the disciple, above even her own sons and daughters, to whom Jesus from the Cross committed the care of His heart-broken mother.

Our Lord at the opening of His ministry had a whole multitude of disciples who followed Him about. But both the needs of His heart and the nature of His work led our Lord to make a selection, and to choose an inner circle of more special friends out of a large and loose multitude. And after much close observation of the conduct and the character of twelve men out of that multitude, and after much prayer, our Lord at last chose those twelve men to have them always with Him. But as time went on, both the drawing of His own heart, and the deeper discovery that the Twelve made of their capacities and their characters, led their Master to make yet another selection of still more special friends, inside the circle even of the Twelve. And thus it comes to pass that, as the Gospels go on from chapter to chapter, we read less and less of the nameless nine, and more and more of the oft-named three: "Peter, James, and John." And then, even of the select three, John more and more stands out as the loved disciple—the special, and peculiar, and by far the most intimate friend of his Master.

The foundation of all friendship is always laid in likeness: in likeness of nature; in likeness of character; in likeness of mind and of judgment; in likeness of tastes, pursuits, and occupations. What certification, then, that is concerning John's mind and character and tastes and pursuits—to be told that, out of all the men that our Lord met with on earth, John was the man He best loved and made His closest friend! And, more than that, "Henceforth I call you not servants," said our Lord, "but I have called you friends, for all things that I have heard of My Father I have made known unto you." Tried by this test also, what a close and intimate friend of his Master John must have been! For, how far beyond all the other disciples, apostles, and evangelists John stands in his knowledge of the things that our Lord had heard of His Father! So far beyond all the other Gospels, in this respect, is John's Gospel, that it reads less like a disciples's writing than an immediate revelation of the things of the Father made to man by the Son Himself. The depth, the inwardness, the heavenliness, the supreme divineness of John's Gospel makes it a perfect miracle of revelation and inspiration. Tried, then, by the test of his Gospel also, how close must have been the likeness, how deep the love, and how perfect the friendship between Jesus and John!

Friendship has had a rich literature all to itself in all ages of the world. But, than Lord Bacon's Twenty-Seventh Essay there has never been anything better written on this fruitful subject of friendship. The study of that matchless piece of writing, taken along with the annotations of its best editors, will throw a flood of fresh and instructive light on this subject which has so much to do with all men's usefulness and happiness. Beginning with the famous passage on Solitude, Bacon goes on with all his superb strength of understanding, and with all his overflowing wealth of illustration, to descant on the two great offices and fruits of Friendship—in relieving the overburdened heart of man; and in clearing up and correcting his confused understanding.

And our own Edward Irving, a great student of the great masters and the great models, has a sermon on this subject not unworthy to stand alongside even of Lord Bacon's Essay. In his fine sermon on friendship, Irving discovers to us the noble office which a good and faithful friend can perform for us in the pilgrimage of this present life. According to Irving, the great office of a friend is to try our thoughts by the measure of his judgment; to task the wholesomeness of our designs and purposes by the feelings of his heart; to protect us from the selfish and solitary part of our nature; to speak to and to call out those finer and better qualities of our nature which the customs of this world stifle; and to open up to us a career worthy of our powers. And lastly, to succour us in our straits, rally us in our defeats, and bind our spirit in its distresses. "Now," adds Iriving, "as every man hath these four attributes—infirmity of judgment, selfishness of disposition, inactivity and inertness of nature, and adversity of fortunes—so every man needeth the help of a friend, and should do his endeavour to obtain one."

1. Well then, that being so, God, our best friend, has appointed us sphere after sphere, and opportunity after opportunity, in which to form friendships, in which to make friends to ourselves, and in which to become the friends of other men. And it is in family life, it is at home and among our own kindred and blood relations, that our first friendships are formed, and our hearts first exercised in those duties and affections in which the life of true friendship has its roots in likeness, the original and primary friendships of the family are laid by nature herself in a deep and essential likeness, out of which the whole rich and various life of human and divine, earthly and heavenly friendships is intended to spring up.

> I, ere thou spak'st,
> Knew it not good for man to be alone…
> What next I bring shall please thee, be assured,
> Thy likeness, thy fit help, thy other self,
> Thy wish exactly to thy heart's desire.

And then, out of this sweet and fruitful likeness and consequent friendship of husband and wife, there spring by God's appointment all the other likenesses and friendships of parent and child, brother and sister, and all our other kith and kin. To honour and obey our parents is the first way, and the best way, to honour and to obey God; and to love, and serve, and give way to, our brothers and our sisters is the divinely appointed path toward loving, and assisting, and acting along with all men as our brethren.

A friend of mine, a minister's son, died lately, who, without the intervention or assistance of tutor or schoolmaster, stepped out of his father's study, already able to face and to take the lead in the full curriculum of even the Aberdeen University. And so is it, so should it be in the moral, social, and religious life of every well-brought-up boy. He should be so exercised and disciplined into the domestic virtues of obedience and submission, self-command, and self-control, respect and reverence, sympathy, wistfulness, and love, that he shall, on his entrance on public life, at once become a power for good, and a pattern and a support of religion and of virtue, wherever his lot is cast. This is what should be; but, alas! It is not always so even in the best of homes, and where one would expect the best of results. It was not so even in that incomparably favoured home in Nazareth, in which Joseph was father, and Mary mother, and Jesus eldest brother. What could it have been that so split up, alienated—not to say embittered—the hearts of that heavenly home? There must have been some fatal lack, somewhere, in that otherwise so happy house. There must have been some sad want of likeness, sympathy, and friendliness somewhere in Joseph's house. Else—why were His brothers and His sisters so blind to our Lord's presence among them—so blind that all Galilee and Jewry believed in Him before His own brothers believed? Else—how could they have eaten at the same table, and gone up to the same synagogue, for thirty years alongside of our Lord, and never have discovered it? Our Lord had to seek His friends outside of His mother's house, and beyond His own blood; else, why were none of His brothers numbered among His disciples? Else, why, when dying on the Cross, did our Lord commit the care of His mother to John and not to her own sons and daughters?

No, family life is not always successful even in the most favourable households. While, again, the very best results are sometimes seen in the most unlikely places.

2. When we are still young and inexperienced and warm-hearted, we think that the life of affection has only to have free scope and full opportunity allowed it in order to turn earth into heaven. Love fills our future ideal home, and friendship fills our future ideal world. But unless we are better taught than that dream, we are doomed to bitter disappointment. Love, real and true love; and friendship, real and true friendship—if they are to become our life companions, and are to abide and be at home with us, must be "rooted and grounded" in us as all our other virtues and graces are rooted and grounded. That is to say, they must be practised and acted on—on principle, and indeed by rule. True love, true friendship, is a habit of mind and heart and will; and like all our other habits of mind and heart and will, our love and our friendship must be built up, drawn out, developed and perfected by constant and studious exercise. A man who would have friends must show himself friendly. He must not take it for granted that his lovers and his friends will stick to him whatever he does to them. He must study the arts and he must live the life of a friend. He must show forethought and take trouble. He must weed out from his heart all those tempers and passions that injure friendship; and he must plant and water all those acts and habits that support and perpetuate friendship. As Dr. Johnson said to James Boswell, he must keep his friendships in constant repair. In an exquisite sermon on this subject, Dr. Newman says: "The real love of man must depend on practice; and therefore it must begin by exercising itself on our friends around us, otherwise it will have no existence. By trying to love our relations and friends, and by submitting to their wishes, though contrary to our own; by bearing with their infirmities; by overcoming their occasional waywardness by kindness; by dwelling on their excellences, and trying to copy them—thus it is that we form in our hearts that root of charity, which, though small at first, will afterwards, like the mustard seed, at last cover the earth."

3. But, not seldom, after all that our homes can give us, and after all that we can do to make friends in our own homes, we have not

seldom to go outside of our own homes for the full satisfaction of our hearts, and for the full assistance and enjoyment of friendship. It was so with our Lord. He had to leave—all unwillingly, we may be quite sure—James and Joses and Simon and Judas behind Him in His mother's house, and go outside to seek His best friends, till, happy for them, He found His best friends in Peter and James and John. Those three happy men afforded our Lord that likeness of mind and heart, that sympathy and that support and that love which His heart craved for, and which His life and His lifework demanded. And so it is sometimes with ourselves. It will sometimes happen that we shall get sympathy, a support, and encouragement, and affection, out of doors, that neither father nor mother, nor sister nor brother, nor wife nor child, can give us. "Thy friend," says Scripture, "which is as thine own soul." There is a climax in the full passage—a climax up which this man's soul is seen climbing, still seeking more and more love. "Thy brother," so the passage runs, "the son of thy mother, or thy son or thy daughter, or the wife of thy bosom, or thy friend, which is as thine own soul."

4. Now, what do you say and what do you think? Suppose you had lived in Galilee in our Lord's day, would He have made you one of His friends? Would you have made Him one of your friends? When chilled at heart, and thrown back upon Himself at home, would Jesus have sought you out till He felt Himself warmed and comforted and restored as He walked the sands of the Sea of Gennesaret with you? Would you have set your other lovers and friends aside to walk with Him? Would He have chosen you to tell you the secrets of His heart? What would you have said to Him when He told you His awful apprehension about Himself, and about the future that His Father seemed to be preparing for Him? What would you have said to your friend when He said to you one Sabbath day coming home from the synagogue: "In the volume of the book it is written of Me"? What would you have talked about by the way as you went up to Jerusalem to the Passover together? Would He have taken you with Him to Jordan to the baptism of John? What would you have done when John pointed you to your old Friend and said, "Behold, the Lamb of God"? And when Jesus, after a night of prayer over

their names, chose twelve—would we have had your name in our New Testament among them? Would He have asked you to sit next to Him at the Passover Supper? Would He have asked you to watch an hour with Him in the garden? Oh, you say, would it have been possible? Is it conceivable? Yes, quite possible, quite conceivable. It is quite conceivable that there are men in this house at this moment who, had their lot been cast in the days of our Lord, would have been found, not only among the Twelve, but among the Three. Do those who are the friends of Jesus Christ, those who have His mind and who do His work—do they seek you out? When dispirited and downcast and alone, do they come to you? Do you minister to them of your substance? Do you share your secrets with them, and do they share their secrets with you? Are you often at their table, and they at yours? And do you all but, as if you were in Jerusalem, take them to your bosom at supper? Whose house are you oftenest in? Whom do you honour and defend with most warmth? Whom, in short, do you most love? I need not say more. By that you will know where you would have been found in Galilee and Jewry. By that you may know where you will be found when Jesus Christ calleth His friends into His Father's house in heaven.

5. "Greater love hath no man than this, that a man lay down his life for his friends." Has this man, then, laid down His life for you? He has, if you have ever asked Him to do it. He has, if you have ever accepted Him as doing it for you. Well, then, *has* He? Do you think He has? Have you any hope that He has? Did you ever ask Him to do it? Did it ever come to this pass with you—either your life or His? And, at that terrible moment, did He say— "I am the sinner's surety: take me and let him go his way"? And ever since that night of substitution and purchase, have you gone your way a redeemed man? When did that transaction between Him and you take place? Where did it take place? Could you show me the spot? How long is it ago? And what manner of man have you been ever since? And, as often as your life has been again and again forfeited, has He interposed again, and again laid down His life for you? Then, you are His friend. If all that is so, you are *His* friend, and He is *your* Friend. And greater love hath no man for any of his friends than this man hath for you.

6. And then, as the dearest friends ought to do—sometimes, and indeed often, tell your friend how much you love Him, for all this as well as for Himself. Though your unkindness and unfaithfulness have been such that it stabs you to the heart to speak about your love to Him alongside of it, yet do it. Trample upon your pride and do it; trample upon your pride and do it; trample upon your shame and do it. Whatever it costs you to do it, do it. Tell Him boldly how much you love Him. "Thou knowest that I love Thee!" retorted Peter, driven half mad with love and with misery, and with his Master's importunity. And still, his Master would have Peter say it, and say it again, and say it again. Nothing would satisfy Peter's Master that day on the sands of the Sea of Galilee but that Peter must say it again and again and again, how much he loved his Master. Commentators and preachers who have no heart in them labour to discover why it was that Jesus asked Peter three times that sweet question. But no man who ever brought his heart with him to that fine chapter ever felt any difficulty with our Lord's hunger for Peter's love, and for the over and over again confession of Peter's love.

"Margaret, never was woman loved so tenderly as thou hast been loved," said a silent husband to his dying wife. "I knew it," was her answer, "I knew it; but I could not die happy till I had heard thee say it. Ah! How I have pined for that sweet word! I had to die to get it, but I do not grudge the price." Say it then to your friend, say it to your husband. And when you have once summoned up strength of heart to say how much you have always loved Him, say it, like Peter, three times. You feel it, and He knows that you feel it; then *say* it. And He will not grudge the price.

12

The Honourable Name

And the disciples were called Christians first in Antioch (Acts 6:26).

"The history of a single word," says a great writer, "will sometimes tell us more than the history of a whole campaign." And the history of this single word "Christians" is the best possible case in point. The word "Christ," from which the word "Christian" comes, was originally a Greek word, and it simply meant one anointed with the holy oil. The first time we meet with holy oil is in the narrative of Jacob's experiences at Bethel. "And Jacob awaked out of his sleep, and he said, Surely the Lord is in this place!… And Jacob took the stone that he had put for his pillows, and set it up for a pillar, and poured oil upon the top of it. And he called the name of the place Beth-el." And from that memorable morning, all down the Old Testament, wherever there was a spot of common earth to be consecrated, or a common man to be set apart and sanctified as a priest, or a sovereign to be enthroned and crowned, Jacob's holy oil was always employed for that sacred purpose. Holy oil came to be one of the most impressive, as well as one of the most universal, of all the sacramental signs and seals in the Old Testament church. And it continued to be so, till all consecration, and all sacrifice, and all sovereignty, came to their consummation in the Christ of God. And thus it is that His Old Testament name, the Messiah, and His New Testament name, the Christ, and His English name, the Anointed One, contain and convey to us the whole heavenly history of His election from everlasting, His predestination, His calling, His consecration, and His complete equipment, in every way, for all the offices He now fills as the incarnate Son of God, and the only redeemer of men. When our Lord first announced Himself to Israel, He opened the

Book, and found the place where it was written of Him: "The Spirit of the Lord is upon me, because He hath annointed me to preach the Gospel to the poor: He hath sent me to heal the broken-hearted, to preach deliverance to the captives, and recovering of sight to the blind, and to set at liberty them that are bruised." This, then, is the true Messiah, the true Christ, the true Anointed, the true and only Christ of God, as the New Testament continually calls Him. Even as Peter opened his mouth, and began to preach Christ to Cornelius and to all his house, in these very words: "how God anointed Jesus of Nazareth with the Holy Ghost and with power, who went about doing good, and healing all that were oppressed of the devil; for God was with Him."

And this is how this great name, "the Christ," came to be given to the man Jesus of Nazareth, above all other men. Almighty God took that chosen man and anointed Him, as never before, with the Holy Ghost. That is to say, God filled the man Jesus of Nazareth as full as human nature could hold of the mind and the spirit, and the grace, and the power, of the Divine Nature. And having so anointed Him, God then presented Him to Israel, and through Israel to the whole world, as the Son of God made flesh, and in His flesh filled with the Holy Ghost. But no sooner was Jesus of Nazareth offered to Israel than that tremendous contention arose which fills the whole of the New Testament—that tremendous contention as to whether Jesus of Nazareth, the carpenter's Son, was indeed the Christ of God or no. We have the whole case and the whole contention put before us in the prayer of Peter and John recorded in the Book of Acts. "The kings of the earth stood up, and the rulers were gathered together against the Lord, and against His Christ. For, of a truth, against thy holy child Jesus, whom Thou hast anointed, both Herod and Pontius Pilate, with the Gentiles and the people of Israel, were gathered together." And that holy and blessed name being then bestowed on God's incarnate Son, in process of time the same name came to be bestowed upon all His disciples, as our present text begins to tell us. I do not know that our first reading of this text would convey to us what all students of the New Testament are agreed upon. That is to say that the name, a Christian, was in the first instance a name of mockery and contempt. It was intended to be an opprobrium and an insult. "Among themselves," says Neander, "they were called the Disciples of the Lord, the Disciples of Jesus, the Brethren, the Believers, and such-like names. The Jews in contempt called them the Galileans, the Nazarenes, the paupers, and such-like names of scorn. But the Jews would, of course, never call them Christians, because that would have been to admit that the Messiah had come, and that these men were His true disciples. But now, when the new religion was spread among the Gentiles, its professors appeared to them to be an entirely new sect, a *genus tertium*, as they were sometimes termed, as being neither Jews nor Gentiles. And as the term Christ was held to be a proper name, the adherents of this new religious teacher were distinguished by a name formed from their master's name, just as the adherents of any school of philosophy were wont to be named after its founder." And as this is both an interesting and an important point, take this also from Trench's *Study of Words*. "What light it throws on the whole story of the Apostolic Church to know when and where this name of Christians was first imposed on the faithful; for, imposed by adversaries it certainly was, not devised by themselves, however afterwards they may have learned to glory in it as the name of the highest dignity and honour. They did not call themselves, but as it is expressly recorded, they were called Christians first at Antioch.... And as it was a name imposed by adversaries, so, among those adversaries, it was plainly heathens and not Jews who were its authors; for Jews would never have called the followers of Jesus of Nazareth 'Christians', or those belonging to the Christ, the very point of their own opposition to Him being that He was not the Christ promised to their fathers, but a false pretender to the name." "Those," says Tacitus, "whom the mob call Christians." Antioch, as we know, was notorious for its jesting and jeering practices; and, strange to say, the noblest name in earth and heaven was first coined in scorn by the jesting mob of Antioch.

Now, from that far-off day in Antioch, this great name has come down through all through all the intervening ages, gathering honour and glory from every new generation of Christian men until, today, we all bear that noblest of names. And until, instead of its being nowadays a jest or an insult to be called a Christian, our only real anxiety about ourselves and about those we love is whether or no we are worthy to bear it—blessed are we above all other men. Whereas, if we bear the name of Christ, and are, all the time, not worthy to bear it, there is no case so sad on the face of the earth as is our case. Let us all examine ourselves, then, in the bright and searching light of this name that we all bear. And then, let us all act according as we discover ourselves to be Christians or no; real and true Christians, or only Christians by name, and no more than by the mere name.

This name, "a Christian," is of such elasticity and liberality in our language that it admits of many senses, and is employed by us every day in many steps and stages of meaning.

To begin with: a child among us is accounted to be a Christian child simply by his birth and his baptism. Already, and before he knows his right hand from his left, or has done either good or evil, but purely in virtue of his birth of Christian parents and his reception into the visible Church by the ordinance of baptism, he already takes the high rank of a Christian child. How he is, eventually, to turn out, whether he is to be a truly Christian man or no, remains to be seen. But by the mere fact of his being born in a Christian home, and then by his visible incorporation into the Christian Church by the sacrament of Baptism, we reckon him a Christian child. The term is employed in this same elastic and liberal way when we speak of the Christian era; when we speak of a Christian land, of Christian civilisation, and Christian art, and so on. Everybody understands and admits the large and loose sense in which this great word is employed in all such cases.

It is a great advance in the proper use of this word when it is still applied to that child when he has risen in years, and in reflection, and in choice, till he is a convinced and a confirmed Christian man.

In both the classes last week, we came on a somewhat startling contradiction, as it seemed to us at first sight, in Dr. Chalmers' estimate of Bishop Butler. To begin with—we found Chalmers early in his ministerial life writing to a friend of his and saying: "It was Butler that made me a Christian." And then, in going through Chalmers' lectures on Butler, delivered far on in his professorial life, we were startled to come on such outspoken condemnations of Butler as these: "Butler's meagre and moderate theology"; "his lax and superficial creed"; "he is entirely devoid of the *sal evangelicum*"; "his is a heart not thoroughly evangelised." We were so staggered by these so contradictory-looking estimates of Butler, and of his services to Chalmers, that we were compelled to go more deeply into Chalmers himself, and into his changed conception of what constituted true Christianity, in order to find, if possible, some explanation of his immense acknowledgements to Butler on the one hand, and his severe censures of the same great man on the other hand. And we found the whole explanation in the fact that Chalmers was employing the word— "a Christian"—in two wholly different senses, in his early correspondence and in his mature discourses. In the former case he was writing as a Christian philosopher; and in the latter case he was speaking as a deeply experienced Christian man. We found that Chalmers' own heart was very far from being "thoroughly evangelised" in the beginning of his ministry, and that, neither in his experience nor in his pulpit, was there a single grain, as yet, of what he afterwards called the *sal evangelicum*. And indeed, there is nothing in our Scottish literature more instructive, and more impressive, than just Dr. Hanna's account of how Dr. Chalmers was led out of his "meagre and moderate" beginnings, and brought into the full light, and life, and power, of evangelical experience. Butler's Christianity was quite enough for Chalmers at one time; but after he had passed through the great change that his son-in-law narrates with such insight and sympathy, it was only then that he became the Chalmers that we all revere and love, and to whom we are all so much indebted. Butler immensely strengthened Chalmers' early hold of Christianity on its intellectual and ethical side. Philosophically and apologetically speaking, Butler may be said to have made Chalmers a Christian in his intellectual convictions, as he has made so many other men. But it is a very impressive and a very illuminating fact that Dr. Hanna applies to Chalmers' early Christianity some of the very epithets of condemnation and complaint that Chalmers' afterwards applied to Butler.

No better illustration could be given of the way that the word "a Christian" penetrates and deepens, from the mind down into the heart, and the will, and the character, than just the case of Dr. Chalmers. His classical Life by Dr. Hanna exhibits with great power the steady deepening, and enriching, and ennobling of a great life and a great ministry, through the steady deepening of his sense of sin and need, and his correspondingly increasing discovery of Jesus Christ as his wisdom, and righteousness, and sanctification. Read and re-read Dr. Hanna's classical Life of Dr. Chalmers.[1]

There used to be a widespread pulpit and private literature among the Puritans of England, and the Presbyterians of Scotland, in which the marks, and evidences, and seals of a truly Christian man were discussed with immense ability and with great enjoyment and profit to the people who were interested in such matters. Baxter's *Saints' Rest* and Brea's *Autobiography* have preserved to this day some first-rate remains of these experimental discussions. If it should be said that our forefathers carried that self-scrutiny much too far, it must be said, on the other hand, that in redressing the balance we have gone much too far the other way. For the most part, we take our Christianity just as it comes to us. We take little or no real trouble to ask ourselves whether we are true Christians or no. We leave all those questions to Him who will make no mistake when He takes our case in hand. But if there should be any one here this morning who has any serious interest as to his own spiritual state in the sight of his Redeemer and his Judge—I can think of no better questions of self-examination than just such as these: What think you of Christ? When do you think of Him? And how often and how long at a time do you think of Him? "I never thought whether there was a Christ or no," confesses John Bunyan in his *Grace Abounding*. Now, "As a man thinketh in his heart, so is he"—that is a true and a time-honoured test.

Then again, what books do you like best? and upon what kind of books and papers do you spend most of your time and your money? I read most in the books I like best. I buy most of the books I like best. I give presents of the books I myself like best. To go no further—if I showed you the books I like best, you would judge quite well as to

---

1 William Hanna, *Memoir of the Life and Writings of Thomas Chalmers, D.D., LL.D.* Edinburgh: Constable, 1852.

whether I am truly a Christian man or no. (That should be said with some reserve, I admit; but to a great extent, and as it touches most men, let us believe that it is not very far from the truth.) And then, as to the pulpit: What books of the Bible do you like best to have opened up to you? And what texts in those books? And what great words and great expressions—say in Paul's Epistles—who was by far the most Christian preacher of all the apostles. What psalms and hymns and spiritual songs do you like best? And what do you oftenest sing to yourself as you lie down and as you rise up? "Read where I first cast my anchor," said John Knox on his deathbed. Where did you first cast your anchor? And where shall we read to you when you are just about to die?

I could risk a good deal, both for you and for myself, on such tests and trials and self-examinations as these. But we are not left to ourselves to seek out our best and surest marks and evidences and tests and trials. The Judge has been good enough, among all His other goodnesses, to foretell us some of the ways in which our Christianity will be tested and tried by Himself on that day. "Not every one that saith unto Me, Lord, Lord, shall enter into the kingdom of heaven: but he that doeth the will of My Father which is in heaven." And again: "Afterward came also the other virgins, saying, Open to us! But He answered and said to them, Verily I say unto you, I know you not." "Then shall the King say unto them on His right hand, Come ye blessed of My Father. For, inasmuch as you did it to one of the least of these My brethren, ye did it unto Me."

"Nevertheless the foundation of God standeth sure, having this seal—The Lord knoweth them that are His."

To sum up, and to sum up in the words of an old writer:

> Four things go to constitute a Christian:
> Faith makes a man a Christian.
> Life proves a man a Christian.
> Trials confirm a man a Christian.
> And death crowns a man a Christian.

May you all be so confirmed and so crowned! Amen!

13

A Great Gospel Text

To him that worketh not, but believeth on Him that justifieth the ungodly, his faith is counted for righteousness (Rom. 4:5).

On Sabbath morning, the 11th of May last, I preached from this pulpit on this selfsame text: "To him that worketh not, but believeth on Him that justifieth the ungodly, his faith is counted for righteousness." I do not know how it has been with you in your own souls all summer, but I can say before you and before God that this glorious Scripture has been my meat and my drink, my strength and my salvation all that time. And such has been my joy in this golden text that I have written my old sermon on it twice over again, during my holiday—so indispensably precious is its truth to me apart from preaching it altogether. And though I were to write this sermon over and over again, every week I live, and were able to preach it again and again to you every Sabbath I live—I would only, in that, be imitating the example and the counsel of the Apostle, who declared that he was determined to know nothing else in his preaching but such apostolical and evangelical doctrine as this.

Well then—once more—Romans chapter four verse five: "To him that worketh not, but believeth...."

It is a strange thing my brethren, and it is a sad thing that it should be so difficult to preach the pure Gospel—to preach the pure, and undiluted, and unadulterated Gospel, and to make it always fresh from the same preacher, and always fresh to the same people. The revivalists keep to the pure Gospel, and they have their reward. But not, for the most part, your educated and ordained and settled preachers and pastors. I only remember once in all my long life hearing this great Gospel text taken up; and it was not by a regular and ordained preacher. It was more than forty years ago; and it was a Professor William Martin, of the Moral Philosophy Chair in Old Aberdeen. I still see the scene, that far-off summer Sabbath evening, on the green lawn before the door of Parkhill House. The Professor's address made an immense impression on me, and on many more besides me, and I have never forgotten it. I may have heard better lecturers on logic and moral philosophy than Professor Martin; but I have never heard better Gospel preaching than his preaching was that sweet Sabbath evening. And his text that evening was these great words of the Apostle: "to him that worketh not, but believeth." Let us also give our whole strength to this great Gospel text this morning.

And, to begin with, "work," as you know, is a word that the Apostle is constantly using. "Work" is almost a technical term in Paul's great evangelical Epistles. Every great science, every great art, every great doctrine and discipline has its own special terminology, its own "technical terms," as we call them. Every new discovery, every new invention, every new doctrine and development of doctrine, demands a new name to describe it, to contain it, and to convey it.

Now, though it is quite true that this word "work" is one of our most familiar words, at the same time, when the Apostle takes that word up into his great Gospel vocabulary, he straightway fills that familiar word of ours with all the fullness of his own inward and profound and spiritual meaning. He fills our word "work" full with such new meanings and with such deep meanings that it takes us days to get at his meanings, and to get this one word of his well into our inexperienced and unspiritual minds.

"To work," in the ordinary and everyday sense of that word, is just to do this and that with our hands. It is to dig, and keep, and dress a garden. It is to plough, and sow, and reap a field. It is to found, and build, and furnish a house. We speak of workshops also, and of workmen, and workwomen. As the Fourth Commandment has it: "Six days shalt thou labour and do all thy work." But there are other and greater commandments than the Fourth, great as it is; and there is far greater work for us all to do than our six days' work, weighty as that work is. "Master," said one in the Gospel, "which is the great

A Great Gospel Text

Commandment in the law?" Jesus said to him: "Thou shalt love the Lord thy God with all thy heart and with all thy strength and with all thy mind; and thy neighbour as thyself."

And thus it is that this greatest and most all-comprehending of all the commandments is laid, not upon our hands only, but upon our hearts; till it embraces and demands for itself, not only all that we do but much more all that we think, and all that we feel, and all that we wish, and all that we desire. Paul's "work," when we come to see it, is every breath we draw; it is every beat of our heart, and every glance of our eye, and every tone of our voice; it is every sigh of ours and every smile. All we are, and all we have, and all we do, must be wholly given up to God and our neighbour, just as God gives up Himself and our neighbour to us. God is love; and love is the fulfilling, both in Him and in us, of God's holy law.

Now, that being so, that being well understood, is it not a very strange thing, is it not a very startling thing, that the Apostle should be found saying here what he does say? That he should actually be found saying in the text that "to him that worketh not," that is to say, to him who loves neither God nor his neighbour aright, such and such great blessings are offered to him, and are indeed pressed upon him. What does the Apostle mean? What can he mean when, after so spiritualising, and so ennobling all our work, he goes on to discharge us from it all and actually to say: "To him that worketh not," such and such indescribable blessings are pronounced and promised? One thing is certain: the Apostle cannot mean what, at first sight, he seems to mean. It is absolutely impossible that the inspired Apostle can mean that the man who does not endeavour, with all his might, to love God and his neighbour, can ever stand accepted before God. No, Paul would be beside himself if he ever said that or anything like that. But as it is, he has the mind of Christ, and he has the message of God to us, when he says—deliberately and authoritatively and conclusively—"To him that worketh not." That is to say, to him who cannot work; to him who, as God is his witness, would work if he were only able; to him who struggles day and night, ay, agonises day and night to do this work and who has given up agonising after anything else; to him who sets God and his neighbour before him continually—but the thing he would do, both to God and to his neighbour, he cannot attain to it. With all his good purposes, and with all his agonising prayers, he cannot attain to it. With all his sweat, and with all his tears, he cannot attain to it. He works his fingers to the bone; he bows his shoulder to the burden; but with it all, and after it all, at the end of every day, he lays down his day's work toward God and man, not only not done, but much further from ever being done than it was when he took it up. Oh, wretched man that he is! Who shall deliver such a helpless and miserable man?

That, then, is how the law of works handles every man who is under the law in this life. And that is how the same law will handle every man when he stands before the bar of God on the day of judgment. "For we know that whatsoever things the law saith, it saith to them that are under the law: that every mouth may be stopped, and all the world may become guilty before God." But what is this? What is this that is here preached to every man whose mouth is stopped? "To him that worketh not," that is to say, as we have seen, who cannot work; to him who, God knows, would work were he only able; "to him that worketh not, but believeth," his faith in God, his faith in Christ, "is counted for righteousness." What is this? What, O ambassador of God unto us—what is this? Tell me, till I clearly understand it, what this new and strange thing believing is? What, with all plainness of speech, is this faith, this believing to which such unheard-of things are everywhere promised?

Well, all true believing, all believing unto life, has in it three distinct steps or stages, the one stage growing out of the other and reposing upon it. The very first step of all believing unto everlasting life is, simply, to believe what is written in the New Testament concerning Jesus Christ. "And many other signs truly did Jesus in the presence of His disciples, which are not written in this book. But these are written that ye might believe that Jesus is the Christ, the Son of God."

But let all our minds be kept the clearest possible at this point on this all-momentous matter. For I may believe what Matthew and Mark and Luke and John write about Jesus Christ—as I believe what Plutarch and Tacitus write about Caesar. That is to say, I may believe my New Testament with what our divines call an "historic" faith. Nay, I might even have stood on Calvary and have seen Jesus Christ on the Cross with my own eyes, and yet might not have gone down to my own house justified. To be justified by faith I must believe that God hath set forth His Son "to be a propitiation through faith in His blood," that God might be just, and the justifier of him that believeth in Jesus. As Walter Marshall has it in his golden *Gospel Mystery*: "The former of these acts of believing doth not immediately unite us to Christ, because it termineth only on the Gospel: yet it is a saving act, so far as it goes, because it instructeth, and inclineth, and disposeth the soul to the latter act whereby Christ Himself is immediately received into the heart. He that believeth the New Testament with hearty love and liking, as the most excellent truth, will certainly with the like heartiness believe on Christ for his salvation." No doubt he will.

And then, true saving faith, being once rooted in any man's heart, it will under the Divine Husbandman's gracious care grow up to the "full assurance of faith" as we see it growing up to full assurance in such great examples of faith, and full assurance, as Abraham in the Old Testament, and Paul himself in the New Testament.

Let all our Gospel preachers, then, be determined not to know anything in this matter among us save this, that "to him that worketh not," that is to say, to him who is absolutely beside himself because the good that he would he does not, and the evil which he would not, that he does; to him who cries out continually, O wretched man that I am!—"to him that worketh not, but believeth on Him that justifieth the ungodly, his faith is counted for righteousness." Do you hear that, O men and women? Do you hear that, O all you who are of all sinners the chief? Do you hear that, O ye saints of His, who are still bearing about with you the body of this death? He with whom you have to do has many names; but His New Testament Name in the text is His best name for you to learn, and to know, and to have always in your mouth and in your heart—even this Gospel Name of His: "Him that justifieth the ungodly." O ungodly man, saint and sinner! Learn, and know continually, this best Name of God for you. It is written in letters of His own blood over the mercy seat. Look up and read it, as often as you again sin. Look up and see Him, where He sits, "that He might be just and the justifier of him that believeth in Jesus." Look up and believe on "Him who justifies the ungodly." "What would I do," exclaimed Dr. Chalmers on his deathbed, "if God did not justify the ungodly?"

Come then, O ungodly man, come! Come just as you are, and "waiting not to rid your soul of one dark blot, to Him whose blood can cleanse each spot." You are a great sinner. Yes, but God sent His Son, not to call the righteous, but sinners, and great sinners, to repentance. It was when every mouth was stopped that God set forth His Son to be a propitiation through faith in His blood. If you were not a great sinner, what justification would God have for not sparing His own Son? He did not send His Son to save small sinners, and those who could save themselves. Man! He came to save you! "Even as David describeth the blessedness of the man to whom God imputeth righteousness without works, saying: Blessed are they whose iniquities are forgiven, and whose sins are covered. Blessed is the man to whom the Lord will not impute sin." "I should be glad to know," wrote Luther in the year 1516 to Spenlein, an Augustinian monk, "I should be very glad to know what is the state of your soul. When you were living with me we were both in this greatest of all errors—seeking to stand before God on the ground of our own works. I am still struggling against that fatal error, and have not even yet entirely triumphed over it. O, my dear brother, learn to know Christ and Him crucified. Beware of pretending to such purity as no longer to confess thyself the Chief of Sinners. If our labours and obediences and afflictions could have given peace to the conscience, why should Christ have died on the Cross? You will never find true peace till you find it and keep it in this—that Christ takes all your sins upon Himself, and bestows all His righteousness upon you." And in 1585, when the Reformation had brought back the English pulpit to the Epistle to the Romans and to the article of a standing or falling Church, Richard Hooker spoke thus in his immortal sermon on Justification. And let his sermon be the cope-stone and crown of mine. "Christ hath merited righteousness for as many as are found in Him. And in Him God findeth us, if we be believers;

for by believing, we are incorporated into Christ. Then, although in ourselves we be altogether sinful and unrighteous, yet even the man who is in himself impious, full of iniquity, full of sin—him being found in Christ through faith, and having his sin in hatred through repentance—him God beholdeth with a gracious eye, and accepteth him in Jesus Christ as perfectly righteous as if he had fulfilled all that is commanded him in the holy law of God; shall I say accepteth him as more perfectly righteous than if himself had fulfilled the whole law? I must take heed what I say; but the Apostle saith: 'God hath made Him to be sin who knew no sin, that we might be made the righteousness of God in Him.' Let it be counted folly, or frenzy, or fury, or whatsoever; it is our wisdom and our comfort. We care for no knowledge in the world but this—that man hath sinned and God hath suffered; that God hath made himself the sin of men, and that men are made the righteousness of God."

"Then said they unto Him, what shall we do, that we might work the works of God? Jesus answered and said to them, This is the work of God, that ye believe on Him whom He hath sent." Amen! For God will bless His own word!

14

The Four Winds

After these things I saw four angels standing on the four corners of the earth, holding the four winds of the earth, that the wind should not blow on the earth, nor on the sea, nor on any tree. And I saw another angel ascending from the east, having the seal of the living God: and he cried with a loud voice to the four angels, to whom it was given to hurt the earth and the sea, saying, Hurt not the earth, neither the sea, nor the trees, till we have sealed the servants of our God in their foreheads (Rev. 7:1–3).

The whole habitable earth is here rolled out into one vast landscape under the eyes of the enraptured seer. Far down beneath his feet, John sees the high mountains and the deep valleys; the broad seas and the rolling rivers; the cornfields and the vineyards; the lonely wilderness and the peopled city. But what takes up the seer's attention, far more than the various spectacle of the outspread earth, is a sight that now comes up upon his vision for the first time. Four mighty angels stand like four living watch-towers on the four corners of the widespread earth. And these four august spirits hold a special command from God to keep sleepless watch and ward at the four great gates of the earth. As the Cherubims stand to keep the way of the tree of life in Paradise, so do these four mighty creatures of God and elect angels of His Son keep the great gates of this beleaguered earth. Storm and tempest, fire and famine, whole seas of trouble rage around and beat up against their close-barred gates; but so vigilant are those four heavenly warders that not so much as one breath of angry air passes through their gates till they open and invite a way. Like wild beasts overmastered and kept at bay, so are all earthly ills kept back by those mighty angels from doing any hurt to those whom they are posted there to protect.

John is still wondering what all that can mean when he sees the four mighty watchmen all at once turn their eyes to the east. And behold, another of those angels who minister to them who shall be the heirs of salvation comes ascending out of the east as the morning sun comes. He comes clothed in light as with a garment; the widespread earth shines bright under his glory; and his voice is as the sound of many waters. Answering to the great keys that the four watching angels hold in their hands, the ascending angel holds in his hand the seal of the living God. And, addressing himself to the four mighty sentinels, he speaks to them with a voice that they hear above all the storms and tempests that war around the earth, saying to them: "Hurt not the earth, neither the sea, nor the trees, till we have sealed the servants of our God in their foreheads."

1. Let it be clearly understood then, and in the first place, that the four winds in this passage are just all those evils to which our life in this world continually lies on all sides open and exposed. For

> Though trouble springs not from the dust,
>   Nor sorrow from the ground;
> Yet ills on ills, by Heaven's decree,
>   In man's estate are found.
>
> As sparks in close succession rise,
>   So man, the child of woe,
> Is doomed to endless cares and toils
>   Through all his life below.

Take the happiest, most hopeful, the most sheltered life among us; but do not suppose that there is any exception there to the universal lot of our human kind. The storm that is predestined to try whether or no that man's house is built on the rock or on the sand—that storm, those winds may be sleeping today like hounds in their couch; but when their master calls for them, they will leap to the chase, and pant after their prey. This earth on which we now stand, and on which we build our houses, is the same earth that John saw surrounded with its waiting storms. You must go out of this world if you would build a house on which no storm will ever beat.

2. The four winds, again, are the very type and emblem, they are the selectest type and the very best emblem, of all that is lawless and uncalculable, capricious, sudden, and unexpected. "The wind bloweth where it listeth, and thou hearest the sound thereof, but canst not tell whence it cometh and whither it goeth." The "large charter" of the wind has become a standing proverb. At the same time, our modern meteorologists do not despair of yet being able to lay a law even on the lawless wind. They intend to discover to us its most secret caves; to calculate its speed and its strength; to lay all its caprices and escapades under rule; and to tell in good time to the sailor on the sea and to the husbandman in the field both whence the wind cometh and whither it goeth. But after all, in all that, we slow-witted men are only learning in the end of the world what God and His guardian angels have known from the beginning. "When He uttereth His voice there is a multitude of waters in the heavens. He causeth vapours to ascend from the ends of the earth; He maketh lightnings with rain; He bringeth forth the wind out of His treasures. O Lord, my God, Thou art clothed with honour and with majesty, who layeth the beams of His chambers in the waters, who maketh the clouds His chariot, who walketh upon the wings of the wind." The storms that rush like infuriated battle-horses over the heads of prostrate men all cease and answer to His call. They all confess His hand. They all sink into silence when He but speaks the word. There is no caprice, there is no lawlessness, there is no suddenness before Him. He says, "Blow!" and straightway becomes a storm. He says, "Peace, be still!" and there is a great calm.

And so is it with the four mystical winds that are under the four mighty angels. Now, they would not waken a sleeping child; and again, they rock the everlasting hills like so many blades of grass. And in calm and in storm alike they are at the command and the permission of God. Not a shadow falls on our threshold but God's hand hung the cloud that casts it in our sky. Not a great wind smites our banqueting-house and makes it the sepulchre of our children, but it was led out of the wilderness under the hand of God. Is there evil in the city, and it has not first had to ask His permission? Has a cedar fallen in the forest, has a hair perished off our head without our heavenly Father? All which is taught us in the noble symbolism of the text when we are let see the angel-warders holding the winds in their fists so that they shall not wantonly, or without permission and command, hurt the earth, or the sea, or any tree. "Are not five sparrows sold for a farthing? And one of them shall not fall to the ground without your Father. Not one of them is forgotten before God. Fear ye not, therefore: ye are of more value than many sparrows."

3. All that is well; all that is wonderful. But best of all is that it is all but the wonderful means to a far more wonderful, and a far more blessed, end. For the four mighty angels, with all their gates, and all their keys, and all their power over wind and sea, over earth and all that earth contains—they are all at the command of that other angel who carries in his hand the sea of God. Hear him, then, as he ascends kindling out of the east. "Hurt not the earth, neither the sea, nor the trees, till we have sealed the servants of God in their foreheads." His errand is to those saints of God who are still upon the earth, and whose sealing is to be carried on and completed under his special care. He is sent forth to minister grace, and to order and to administer providence to all those saints and servants of God who are being specially and speedily sealed for their translation to heaven, and for their presentation without spot or blemish before God in love. This angel who has the seal looks on all God's saints on earth with eyes that see their hidden saintliness: the true nature of it, the exact stage of it, and just what it still wants to perfect it, as well as just when and how its full perfection is to be accomplished. And, as the angel with the seal communes with and gives his commands to the four angels of the winds, we come to see how grace commands and is supreme over providence; and how the angels of providence rejoice to subserve the angel of grace and of a sealed holiness. Earth, in this view, takes all her orders immediately from heaven; and heaven again takes her orders from Him who has the seven-sealed Book in His hand. All earth's gates—her north gate and her south gate, her east gate and her west gate—they all wait, are all opened and shut, are all shut and opened at the word of the angel with the seal. The great gateways of the earth are filled with hurrying feet; and again, they are silent as the grave, just as he signifies it is to be. Every door that lets

in joy and sorrow on the sons of men, and especially on the saints and servants of God, he keeps the key of it. The four great watchmen wait for his descent and his signal more than they watch for the morning.

At the same time, masterful and clothed with authority as this angel is, he does not say, he does not assume, that he seals all God's servants in his own strength and in his own office alone. No, he takes all his four brethren along with him. He looks to them as much as they look to him. He acknowledges them; he claims them and counts on their co-operation. "Till we," he says, "till we have sealed God's servants." The ascending angel carries the seal; but the four stationary angels, the four storm-gate guardians, are his assistants and his fellow-workers, and are indeed his indispensable forerunners. They make ready his sealing work for him. He comes but to gather up and to finish what they have begun and carried up and to finish what they have begun and carried so far on. For we know now that these powerful four are they who with their four winds surround our lives with awaking, alarming, arresting, and sanctifying providence. These are they who warn us not to build our nest in any forest on the earth. These are they who speed up and down and overrule our own world of tribulation. These are they whose blessed ministry all the saints celebrate with that psalmist who said that it had been very good for him to be afflicted. These are they whose ministry of trial and tribulation did so much for Job and for Jonah in the Old Testament, as well as for our Lord Himself and for all His apostles in the New Testament. "Hurt not the earth," said the angel from the east, "till we, the angels of providence and of grace, have sealed the servants of our God in their foreheads."

4. But, "the seal of the living God"—what, just what is that? What is it but, so to say, the Royal Signet-ring of Heaven? That seal has been worn on the arm of the King Eternal, Immortal, and Invisible, ever since that day when the only wise God, to Whom be honour and glory for ever and ever, first chose a people for Himself. He set it then as a seal upon His heart, till all His covenant people should be gathered in and brought home in holiness and in love. That seal bears on its face an image that no earthly artificer can counterfeit. For its secret device is the perfect image and likeness of Jesus Christ,

the Son of God, and its signature is the new covenant name of the Father Himself. And that the ascending Angel has that seal in his hand shows us what an Angel he is, how much he is trusted, what a rank he holds, and on what an errand he is sent out. It shows, also, the surpassing grace that comes to that servant of God on whose forehead this angel sets this seal. For, when set on any man's forehead, it certifies Heaven and Earth and Hell whose that man henceforth is. "He is Mine," says Almighty God before Heaven and Earth and Death and Hell. "I have loved him with an everlasting love. I have called him by his name and he is Mine. I have redeemed him. I have justified him. I have adopted and I have sanctified him. He is Mine. He is Mine. He is Mine."

And the setting of this seal on the forehead of a saint of God on earth is the last—the last and the supreme act of Divine Grace upon that saint till grace rises above itself and becomes glory.

(1) Now, there are some secret legends graven on and suspended from the great seal of the King of Glory—secret legends that we should all have transcribed upon our hearts. And "Dear in God's sight is the death of His saints" is one of those legends. That fine legend is to be read in letters of deepest gold on that splendid seal. Yes, dear to God is that day, because He knows all that that day is, and is to be to Him and to His saints; and that day is dreadful and not dear to us just because we are still on the earth and not yet with John in heaven. For that day, like every day, has two sides—an earthly side and a heavenly. The day of the death of one of God's saints is only called death on earth. On earth, for it is the day of their final deliverance; it is the day of their full coronation; it is the day of their deathless life in heaven. The last touch the sealing angel puts to a saint's forehead on earth may be put amid storm and tempest and a great darkness. It often is. It always is. The angel with the seal descends to perfect his work on the wings of the storm-wind. And that wind, as if to pay its last debt to that saint's house, as if to deliver its last blow to that saint's awakening, and to the sorrow that has been his salvation—that wind makes all things rock and reel beneath him and around him on the day of his death as never before. But that is just because this is the last time the sealing angel is to descend on

that saint's house; this is the last service also of those four angels to this saint till they return to the throne to give in their account.

And thus it is that while we are wringing our hands and are charging God and His guardian angels foolishly, He is saying to those same angels, "Well done!" and to His saints, "Come hither, ye blessed!" Yes, dear in God's sight is every day of His saints; but dear above all other days is the day of their last sealing on earth, and their "abundant entrance," and their unblemished presentation before His throne in heaven.

(2) "He shall give His angels charge over thee, to keep thee in all thy ways"—that also is graven on the Divine Seal; and from thence that is written on the heart of every much-experienced saint of God. Yes, assuredly. Each several saint of God as he goes on in his life of sanctification comes to accumulate many such records of special providences, miraculous interpositions, times of storm that carried angels to his house on the wings of the wind, till his house is well watched as John saw the whole earth watched. And that goes on till we cannot return to any house we have ever lived in, we cannot revisit any past period of our life, without being compelled to say—*there* and *there* and *there* He gave His angels charge over me! I saw it then! and ten times clearer I see it now! And, blessed be His name, in a thousand ways He calls that past to our mind, and assures us that our thankful mind is true and right. And that goes on, the secret of the Lord increasing with them that fear Him, till, behold, at every corner of our house we see an angel stationed every night; and till we cannot come out at our closet door but we see the sheen of the seal in the midnight sky.

(3) But the very foundation and substance of God's seal, and the oldest and the deepest of all the things that are engraven upon it is this: that the will of God is our sanctification. And till I begin to see that on God's seal, and till I begin to feel the imprint of that upon my forehead, all my life in this world is a vast maze without any meaning to me. It is a dark labyrinth now! There is the key to the whole mystery now! There is something for me to live for, and, if need be, to suffer all my days for now! There is something not unworthy of the interest of angels in me and in my affairs now! Nay, worthy of the

Lord of all angels Himself! I look back and see it all now. All God's vast patience with me, and all His marvellous providences over and all about me, are as plain as day now! Sanctification! Sanctification! A sealed and an accepted sanctification! Sweetest of words! Most blessed hopes! O! Blessed will of God with me! And blessed angels, both of providence and of grace, who have had even a ministering hand in such a sanctification as mine shall be! But, blessed far above all speech on earth, and above all song in heaven, that sinner, that saint, that servant of God, on whose sanctification and sealing will of God has been from all eternity set!

PART THREE
In Remembrance of Me

15

The Comforts of God

Comfort ye, comfort ye My People, saith your God (Isa. 40:1).

"The boundless exhilaration" of Isaiah is a proverb in sacred letters. There is nothing anywhere else in literature, sacred or profane, to compare with the hope, the joy, the rapture, the transport of Isaiah. The book of Revelation itself—that so transcendent book—goes back and borrows some of its most captivating visions, as well as some of its sublimest language, from the book of Isaiah. The New Testament has so completely taken over into itself this Old Testament book that it is impossible for us to read this book any more simply as Isaiah wrote it.

When we read of Babylon in Isaiah, we immediately think of our own bondage to sin. When we read of Cyrus, we have already forgotten Cyrus, because we have seen Christ. When our students study "the Servant of the Lord" in Isaiah, their hearts turn to their Saviour, and they say to Him: "Lo, now speakest Thou plainly, and speakest no parable. For Thou hast in very deed been wounded for our transgressions, and bruised for our iniquities, and the Lord hath laid on Thee the iniquity of us all." And when we read in the eloquent prophet how the wilderness was transformed into the garden of the Lord around the returning exiles, it is far more wonderful, and far more eloquent to us—the way the Lord is leading ourselves. Nor can we read Isaiah's noble description of his and his people's New Jerusalem without our heart melting within us to be for ever home in the Jerusalem which is above, which is free, and which is the mother of us all.

No fewer than twenty-seven chapters of Isaiah's great book are taken up with the comfort of the captives in Babylon. And large and evangelical as is the scope, rich and far-reaching as is the vision, and surpassingly eloquent as is the style of those twenty-seven chapters—at the same time every word of those chapters is spoken and written for the comfort of the captive people. And the "incomparable exhilaration" of those twenty-seven chapters is all due to this: that "the God of all comfort" not only gives Isaiah his commission of comfort, but puts the very comforts themselves, as well as the very words in which those comforts are to be described, into the prophet's mouth. The God of Israel rises up to comfort His people Himself in this golden book. Only, He conveys those comforts through the golden heart and the golden mouth of this greatly-gifted and greatly-graced prophet. So much have we of God Himself in this book, and so little of Isaiah, beyond his name and his voice, that we may take this book as all but the speech and the penmanship of the Divine comforter Himself, carrying out His own command: "Comfort ye, comfort ye My people. Speak ye comfortably to Jerusalem; speak to her heart."

Supper being ended, when Jesus knew that His hour was come that He should depart out of this world to the Father, He set Himself to comfort His sorrowing disciples. When Simon Peter said to Him, "Lord, whither goest Thou?" Jesus answered him: "Let not your heart be troubled: ye believe in God, believe also in Me. In my Father's house are many mansions: I go to prepare a place for you. And if I go and prepare a place for you, I will come again and receive you to myself: that where I am, there ye may be also." And when Thomas raised this difficulty, "Lord, we know not whither Thou goest; and how can we know the way?" Jesus comforted Thomas with these great words: "I am the Way, the Truth, and the Life." And when Judas raised *his* difficulty, "Lord, how is it that Thou wilt manifest Thyself to us, and not to the world?" his Master explained to him: "If a man love Me, he will keep My words; and My Father will love him, and We will come unto him and make Our abode with him." And then, from that, our Lord passed on to promise and to describe the Holy Ghost as "Another Comforter," whom the Father will send to them in answer to His prayer. And it is of the first importance to every New Testament disciple to have ever before him the very words in which our Lord describes and promises the Holy Ghost. "I will pray the Father, and He will give you another Comforter, that He may abide with you for ever. And ye know Him: for He dwelleth with you, and shall be in you. The Father will send the Comforter in My name, and He shall teach you all things and bring all things to your remembrance, whatsoever I have said to you. It is expedient for you that I go away: for if I go not away, the Comforter will not come unto you; but if I depart, I will send Him to you. He shall guide you into all truth. He shall take of Mine and shall show it unto you. These things I have spoken unto you, that in Me ye might have peace. In the world ye shall have tribulation: but be of good cheer; I have overcome the world."

1. Now, in passing on to apply all that to ourselves, the first thing is to raise the question whether this comfort, or any part of it, belongs at all to us. "Comfort ye, comfort ye *My people*, saith your God." "The world cannot receive the Comforter," says our Lord, "because it seeth Him not, neither knoweth Him." The Holy Ghost is sent to the world indeed, but not as a Comforter. "When He is come," says our Lord, "He will reprove the world of sin, and of righteousness, and of judgment." Now, has He so come to *you*? Has He been so received by you? Do you receive and accept His reproofs of sin? Do you hunger after the righteousness He holds up before you? Do you humble yourself under the judgment He passes on you? As you do so, and in the measure you do so, and at times you do so, to that extent and at those times you pass over from the world which knoweth not the Spirit of truth, and you gain the discipleship to which their Master sends the Comforter. Has He, then, the Reprover and the Sanctifier, come to you, and been received by you? That is the first question. That is the *previous* question. Not that it need be feared that the world will be greedy to take to itself the comforts of God's people. It "cannot," says our Lord. For it neither sees those comforts nor knows them. No more it does, when you think of it. What could a man of Babylon have made of the Prophecy of Isaiah? Even the wisest of the men of the East, what could they have made of the evangelical prophet? He would have been "foolishness" to them. They had not, as Paul would say, the mind of Christ. They had not had the experience of a true Israelite. Babylon was no banishment to them. Jerusalem had no attractions to them.

Nay, not only had Jerusalem and her prophets and her promises no attractions to the men of Babylon, there were many men of Israel who turned a deaf ear to the prophet's comforts. It is a matter of history that multitudes of Israelites remained in Babylon, and would not face the wilderness, in spite of all that Isaiah and his fellow-prophets could say. And so it is still. The iron has not sufficiently entered our hearts. The bondage has not sufficiently broken our hearts. The Holy Ghost has not sufficiently come as a reprover of sin and of righteousness and of judgment; and as a consequence we are not prepared for Him as a Comforter. "That the saying of Esaias the prophet might be fulfilled, which he spake, Lord, who hath believed our report? and to whom hath the arm of the Lord been revealed?"

2. The first difficulty that the Holy Ghost has with us is to get His reproof of sin, and His conviction of sin, brought home to our hearts. And then, that accomplished only raises another difficulty: how to get His *comforts* spoken in our reproved and convicted hearts. The captives, whose hearts and consciences were in the Babylonian captivity, raised as many doubts, difficulties, apprehensions and obstacles in Isaiah's way as the disconsolate disciples did in their Master's way—till Isaiah's answers, till God's answers to their guilty and fearful hearts have made Isaiah as good as an apostle of Christ, as good as a preacher of New Testament consolation. You all know these golden consolations. "I, even I, am He that blotteth out thy transgressions for Mine own sake, and will not remember thy sins. I have blotted out, as a thick cloud, thy transgressions, and as a cloud thy sins: return unto Me, for I have redeemed thee. Look unto Me, and be ye saved, all the ends of the earth: for I am God, and there is none else. For a small moment have I forsaken thee: but with great mercies will I gather thee. In a little wrath I hid My face from thee for a moment; but with everlasting kindness will I have mercy upon thee, saith the Lord thy Redeemer." These are God's very own words to us this morning. To all of us, that is, who have come up to this house reproved and convinced of sin. "Comfort ye, comfort ye My people, saith your God. Speak ye comfortably to Jerusalem, and cry unto her, that her seventy years are accomplished, and that her iniquity is pardoned!"

3. But, let this be said in the same breath with all that, this caution and correction: that no man living in any known sin is ever comforted of God. The Holy Ghost never yet spake one word of all His abounding consolations to any man so long as he lived in any actual sin, or in any neglect of known duty. You have that much-needed caution bound up into the very heart of God's great name, when He proclaimed His great Name to Moses. "The Lord God, merciful and gracious, long-suffering, and abundant in goodness and truth, keeping mercy for thousands, forgiving iniquity and transgression and sin, *but*"—and here comes this great correction and caution—"will by no means clear the guilty." That is to say, as long as you are living in any *guilt*, as long as your conscience accuses you, He will by no means clear or comfort you. "He that forsaketh his sin shall find mercy"—but he only. You do not really care for God's mercy or His comfort either, so long as you live in any sin. And it is well that you do not, for you can have neither. Your peace will be like a river when you put away your sin; but not one word of true peace, not one drop of true comfort, can you have till then. You will have to put out God's eyes and pervert His judgment and turn His Throne upside down before you can have His comfort with your sin. Choose which you will have: "If a man love Me, he will keep My words: and My Father will love him, and We will come unto him, and make Our abode with him." Are *you* that man? Are you intending to be that man? And when and in what are you to begin? Are you from this day to keep that word of His, which up to this day you have not kept? Then, from this day Jesus and His Father will come to your good and honest, if broken and contrite heart, and will make Their abode with you. And from this memorable day it will be said over you from heaven, what was said from heaven in Israel over all the men in Israel like you: "To this man will I look, saith the Lord, even to him that is poor and of a contrite spirit, and who trembleth at My word."

4. This is the rule, then: that comfort comes with obedience. But there are exceptions to every rule; and God's rules with His people are full of exceptions. His people are so full of idiosyncrasy, non-conformity, and originality that no rule could possibly be laid down that would cover them all, or indeed, any two of them all. And hence

it is that God has to make as many rules in His sanctification and comfort of His people as He has people to sanctify and comfort. Every new addition made to God's people has a new rule made for itself. Heman[1] and Job are great favourites with the profounder of the Puritan case-preachers. Heman and Job were famous exceptions to the common rule that comfort comes with obedience. And you may possibly be a New Testament Job or Heman. You may, like them, have been chosen of God on a special platform on which God is going to display some deep and sovereign exception to His usual manner of dealing with His people. That may be so; but you will be well advised not to assume that too much till you have proved it true by a lifetime of strict and spiritual obedience. And then, if, after a lifetime of strict and spiritual obedience, you are still left without your promised and expected comfort, why then you are in good company, and must not complain. "God gives grace," says Goodwin, "in cases where He does not give comfort; and then, He is the God of all grace in a far larger extent than of all comfort: yea, and often He gives most grace when He gives least comfort. He carries on some souls—as He carried on Christ at His death—that is, to the highest acts of obedience, whilst yet He vouchsafes no comfort. Witness that doleful expression of Christ: 'My God, My God, why hast Thou forsaken Me?' when yet He was in the highest act of obedience. Thus in thy temptation God will influence thee with grace, secretly assisting and strengthening thee, even when He affords thee no sensible comfort." "Carry this home with thee," adds the great preacher comfortably—"Carry this home with thee, thou who hast for so many years been tossed with tempest and not comforted."

5. "Oh," some of you will say in answer to all that. "You speak of exceptions, but I am an exception in nothing but in the corruption of my heart. How could God or man comfort a heart like mine? No man sees my heart, else all men would flee from me. And it is because God sees my heart that He has so forsaken me. Do not speak about comfort to me! I want no comfort. I want—if God would give it and could give it—I want a clean heart; *that*, as God is my witness, would be comfort enough for me. I want the devil and hell taken out of my

---

1 See the title of Psa. 88.

heart," you protest. Your only moments of comfort are not when your corn and wine abound, but when the devil is asleep for a season. "O, wretched man that I am! I am of all men the most miserable!" Yes! and No! You *are;* and you are *not*. I will tell you a far greater misery than yours, and a far greater wretchedness. It is a great deal worse misery to be miserable and not to know it. To be poor, and miserable, and blind, and naked, and to think all the time that you are rich and increased with goods and have need of nothing. At your worst, that is not your misery. If to know your misery is any alleviation of it, then surely that alleviation is yours. If to know nothing but misery is any preparation for God's mercy—as it is—then according to your own showing and out of your own mouth, who among us all is prepared for God's mercy this day like you? There is only one Scripture you ever get any comfort out of. This is your text every morning, and you come back to it every night. "The good that I would, I do not," you say, "but the evil which I would not, that I do." Very good. But, come on! Come on, and complete your own Scripture: "I find, then, a law that when I would do good, evil is present with me." And come on still: "For I delight in the law of God after the inward man. O wretched man!" you cry of your own accord, yes; but there is more: "I thank God through Jesus Christ my Lord. There is therefore now no condemnation." And ere ever you are aware, you will be swimming in a sea of comfort, a sea without a bottom or a shore. You are launched upon the eighth of the Romans, and into the ocean of comfort, out of which that great chapter is but a cup.

6. You would let go; you would yield yourself up on the spot to any of God's comforts He or His servants are pleased to speak to you this day, if it were not that you are such an atheist and scandal in prayer. But your conscience is so in prison about prayer that you feel as if you must flee from the Lord's table. Bad as your heart is, and bad as your life has been, yet there is nothing that makes you feel so despicable and so castaway as your shameful neglect of prayer. You like to read books about prayer. You like to hear sermons about prayer. You revere and love the men of prayer. But all that only makes you a greater beast before God. You are in positive despair about prayer. And yet, you know on the testimony of thousands, and on

the assurance of God's Word in endless places, that prayer is, of all things a mortal man can perform, by far the most blessed. How can prophet, or apostle, or the Holy Ghost Himself, comfort you? You refuse to be comforted! The greatest and the best of comforts is in your own house, is every day, morning and night, and seven times a day, in your own heart; and you will not move a hand or foot to take it. There is no mystery about prayer—no mystery, but its nearness, and its easiness, and its sureness, and its fruitfulness, and its supreme, immediate, and everlasting blessedness. Only begin to pray. Prayer, of all things, only needs a beginning. Begin, and it will beat you to give over. Begin, and you will be a man of prayer yourself before you know where you are—a man of power with God, and not only a greatly comforted man yourself, but a fountainhead of comfort to many others. What a father you would then begin to be and what a mother! What a sister and what a brother! What a friend; what a lover! What a minister and what a member! For you would have a well of comfort springing up in your own heart; and out of your heart comfort would flow like a river, far and near round about you. Till you, even you would be found exclaiming with Paul: "God comforteth us in all our tribulation, that we may be able to comfort them that are in any trouble, by the comfort wherewith we ourselves are comforted of God." "You will comfort My people," saith your God to His servants, "if you could prevail with them to pray." We shall do our best, O God! Only pour out on us all, prophets and people, the promised spirit of prayer and supplication!

7. But the Lord's Supper is the crown and the seal of all our best comforts in this life. And you will never be nearer the "God of all comfort" till you sit down with Him in heaven, than you will be immediately, in a few moments. "I sat," says the Bride, "under His shadow with great delight, and His fruit was sweet to my taste. He brought me into His banqueting-house, and His banner over me was love."

> Thou art coming to a King;
> Large petitions with thee bring:
> For His grace and power are such,
> None can ever ask too much.

16

The Evangelical Prophet

Who hath believed our report? (Isa. 53:1).

It was when Jerome was engaged in translating this chapter out of its original Hebrew into his western Latin that he exclaimed in wonder and in praise: "Surely this is the chapter of a New Testament evangelist, rather than of an Old Testament prophet!" And ever since Jerome said that, Isaiah has been known in the Church as the Evangelical Prophet. "Not only many Jews," says Albert Bengel, "but even atheists have been converted to Jesus Christ by means of this chapter. History records the names of some of them: God alone knows the names of them all." And John Donne says that as "in the New Testament we have 'The Gospel according to Matthew,' and 'The Gospel according to Mark,' and 'The Gospel according to Luke,' and 'The Gospel according to John,' so in the Old Testament we have 'The Gospel according to Isaiah.'" "The fifty-third of Isaiah," says Delitzsch, "reads as if it had been written beneath the Cross of Calvary. This chapter is the most central chapter, the deepest and the highest chapter, in the whole of the Old Testament. The Holy Ghost has here excelled Himself," says Delitzsch.

And indeed, this most wonderful chapter deserves all, and more than all, that has ever been said in admiration of it. The Old Testament believers cast their surest anchors on this Scripture. They had more anchorages than this; but this was the surest, the safest, and the most consoling anchorage of them all. There is nothing, indeed, like this chapter even in the New Testament itself. There is no other single Scripture in the whole of the Word of God in which the sin-atoning death of the Son of God is set before the faith of a sinner as it is here. Simply nowhere else is the redeeming death of Christ set forth so clearly, so fully, so emphatically, so explicitly, so positively, so experimentally, so impossibly-to-be-disputed, and so impossibly-to-be-for-one-moment-doubted—as it is here. A sinner must have his eyes sealed up very close indeed not to see his salvation here. He must surely have a very seared conscience who does not flee to the Cross of Christ as it stands so open to him in this chapter. Listen again to the accumulated statements of the atonement in this single Scripture; listen, and cast your anchor on every one of them, as I repeat them to you for that purpose. "He hath borne our griefs, and carried our sorrows. He was stricken, smitten of God, and afflicted. He was wounded for our transgressions; He was bruised for our iniquities; the chastisement of our peace was upon Him; and with His stripes we are healed. All we like sheep have gone astray; we have turned every one to his own way; and the Lord hath laid on Him the iniquity of us all. He was oppressed, and He was afflicted, yet He opened not His mouth. He is brought as a lamb to the slaughter, and as a sheep before her shearers is dumb, so He openeth not His mouth… For the transgression of my people was He stricken… It pleased the Lord to bruise Him; He hath put Him to grief. When Thou shalt make His soul an offering for sin… He shall bear their iniquities… because He hath poured out His soul unto death; and He was numbered with the transgressors; and He bare the sin of many, and made intercession for the transgressors."

All the other Scriptures of the Old Testament are written with pen and ink; but these things read as if they were written with the very blood of Christ Himself, with the sin-atoning blood of the Lamb of God slain for Old Testament believers and New, before the foundation of the world.

"The Lord hath laid on Him the iniquity of us all." Could any conceivable language be clearer? What more, what better for us could possibly have been said? Nothing better, unless it is the margin, where it is said: "The Lord hath made the iniquity of us all to meet on Him." Now, my brethren, though it is not too much for Almighty God and His Divine Son to take up and deal with the iniquity of us all, it is impossible for us to take up all that iniquity into our minds and to lay it all upon our hearts. And it is not intended, nor expected, that we should do so. What we are called to think and to deal with here is our own individual iniquity, and to think of it as taken off us and laid upon Jesus Christ. We shall simply lose ourselves, we shall simply drown ourselves, if we begin with the iniquity of all other men, and try to wade out into that ocean, and into our Lord's atoning death for all that. The right way is to begin and end with our own iniquities, and with our Lord's atoning death for us and for them. The right way is to read this great Scripture as if it were written for, and addressed to, each single one of us separately and alone, and as if there were no other sinful man for Christ to die for in the whole world but ourselves. "Hast thou believed our report?" This demand is made to each one of us, severally and alone. "Has the arm of the Lord been revealed to thee? Has the Lord made all thine iniquities to meet on His substituted Son?" The whole Atonement—in all its length, and breadth, and height, and depth—is far too high and far too deep for us. It is enough for us to have to make sure that our own iniquities have all been atoned for, and that the Son of God has taken them all for ever away, and has given us His own justifying righteousness in their place.

And as it is our own sin and iniquity that we are to think of when the report of the atonement is made to us, even so it is certain particular sins and transgressions of our own that we are to think of. We are not to attempt to think of the mass and the immensity of our sins, for that also is far too much for us. A long lifetime of sin, and then our whole nature steeped and soaked in sin—what human mind could keep all that in memory or could ever take up and feel aright the full weight and guilt and shame of all that? No human mind, no human heart could ever do so. It is absolutely impossible. But it is possible to take this and that sin, this and that transgression, and lay it on our offered Surety and Substitute. "Innumerable evils compass us all about," and pursue us like so many avengers of blood. But it is not our innumerable evils that we are always to deal with, so much as that evil, and that evil, and that other evil, committed at that time, and at that place, and against that person, God or man. It is this and that particular evil and special sin that we are to fix our eyes on, as the Lord takes it and lays it on His sin-bearing Son.

And then, when we do that, how our sins horrify us at such times, and make us at such times to hate them almost as much as God Himself hates them! To have to take this and that sin, in all it vileness and wickedness, and to have to stand and see it taken off ourselves and laid on the sinless head of the Son of God. Oh, brethren, why does that not break our hearts in pieces, never to be healed again? Why does that not make it impossible for us ever to perpetrate that sin again? Oh, the fearful dominion of sin! Oh, the unspeakable deceitfulness and persistence of sin! That it can still survive such awful experience as that! And that it can still steal away our hearts from such a God and such a Saviour! But hard and all but hopeless as our hearts are, yet every time we do attempt to take such and such a sin and to lay it on Another, and on such Another, as a matter of fact that does do something to horrify our hearts at that sin, and at the thought of loading and defiling and crucifying the Son of God again with that sin. But in His mercy, God tempers and softens our sight of our sin, and of His Son's death for our sin; else we would lose our reason at the awful sight. All the same, soften it as He may, it remains absolutely true—as true as God is true; as true as Christ is true; as true as the Gospel is true—that the Lord hath laid on Him all our iniquities, all the most abominable, and the most aggravated of our iniquities and our transgressions.

And then, what a cruel catalogue of our Lord's sufferings for our sins this prophet here reads home upon our broken hearts! "His visage, marred more than any man, and His form more than the sons of men. Stricken, smitten, wounded, bruised, chastised, scourged, oppressed, afflicted." And every accursed syllable of all that: "for me." Nothing of all that would ever have come near Him, but for me. All that was my desert. All that was the wages of my sin. But for Him, and His interposition, and His substitution of Himself, my visage would have been marred more than any man. But for Him, I would have been despised and rejected of men, and no man would ever have put any esteem upon me. I would have been stricken, smitten of God, and afflicted. I would have been wounded, and bruised, and chastised, and scourged. I would have had all mine iniquity laid on myself. I would have been oppressed and afflicted; I would have been bruised and put to grief! That, communicants, is the way for you and me to go through this expiation-Scripture. That is the way for a man to examine himself and so to eat of that bread and drink of that cup. That is the way to "receive the atonement." That is the way so to make Christ our sin that we may be made His righteousness. That is the way to let Him see of the travail of His soul, that it has not been wholly lost and altogether thrown away upon us. "I, O Esaias! I, for one, have believed thy report! To me, for one, has the arm of the Lord been revealed!"—so let us all say, and each man for himself.

Among the many amazing things of which this amazing chapter is full, there is nothing that arrests us, and overawes us, and, indeed, staggers us more than this—that it "pleased the Lord to bruise" His Messiah-Son. But the simple truth of God in this matter is this. God was so set, from everlasting, on the salvation of sinners that the most awful steps that had to be taken in order to work out that salvation are here said to have absolutely pleased Him. It is somewhat like our Lord's own words: "I delight to do Thy will"—even when His Father's will led Him to the garden of Gethsemane and the Cross of Calvary. God so loved the world that He gave up His only-begotten Son to die for the sin of the world. God could not be pleased with the death of His Son—in itself. No. But nothing has ever pleased Him more than that His Son should lay down His life in atonement for those sinners whom the Father had chosen and ordained to everlasting life. Paul has everything. And he has the Father's indebtedness to His Son and His good pleasure in His death in this great passage: "God hath set forth Christ Jesus to be a propitiation through faith in His blood: to declare His righteousness, that He might be just and the justifier of him which believeth in Jesus." It pleased the Lord to bruise Him, because in this way alone could God's full hatred of sin be declared to men and angels, and at the same time God's justice might be manifested in the salvation of sinners. Yes, "Esaias is very bold" when he says that "it pleased the Lord to bruise Him." But in saying that, Esaias is not one word bolder than is the whole of the glorious Gospel in its proclamation of God's supremest glory in the death of Christ, and in the consequent salvation of sinners, and a multitude of such that no man can number. As one of the greatest preachers of the Gospel that ever lived has it: "For God to deliver up His Son to death, and for Himself to bruise Him, and that this should be His good pleasure, there must have been some incomprehensibly vast design of glory to accrue therefrom and to be only attained by doing it—some high end, and far transcending design, that was to be the issue and the product of it; and which, as you know, was the manifestation and magnifying of His grace in the salvation of sinners. And this is surely the very highest evidence and argument to our faith that can possibly be given: that God is determined to save sinners. For what has been done to Christ is for ever past recalling, and is not to be justified or recompensed in any way other than by saving many by the knowledge of Him—as God here speaks by the mouth of His prophet."

"Yet it pleased the Lord to bruise Him: He hath put Him to grief: when Thou shalt make His soul an offering for sin, He shall see His seed, He shall prolong His days, and the pleasure of the Lord shall prosper in His hand." Now this is the conclusion of the whole matter, for this morning: Does He see His seed in us? In you and in me? If He does, then He is "satisfied" for all the "travail of His soul" so far as we are concerned. He forgets and forgives all His sufferings when He sees His seed; when He sees the souls He has redeemed to God with His own blood, putting on His image, and filled with His Spirit, and continuing His work in this world. Now, in closing, let us look back into this great chapter as into a glass, in order to see if we can recognise any of the features and characteristics of Christ in ourselves, any of those features and characteristics of Christ as they are here so impressively set forth to our faith, and to our love, and to our imitation. As thus: "He is despised and rejected of men: a man of sorrows and acquainted with grief: He was despised and we esteemed Him not." Now as to the bearing of all that upon us, the Apostle Peter has spoken to all time. And this is what he has said: "For hereunto were ye called, because Christ also suffered for us, leaving us an example, that ye should follow His steps, who, when He was reviled, reviled not again. When He suffered, He threatened not." Now, how do you stand in these matters? For, every day and every hour, God so orders things around some of you, and so brings things to bear upon some of you, that you are buffeted and reviled and despised and rejected almost every day. And that for this very purpose: that at such times Christ shall see His seed in you. Now, does He? You know your own heart under all that discipline; and He knows it. Now, does He see in your heart at such times of temptation and trial a copy of His own? "A copy, Lord, of Thine."

Then again, you will sometimes be wounded for other people's transgressions, as He was for yours. And "bruised for their iniquities," as He was for yours. Now, how about your speech or your silence under all that? "He opened not His mouth." How happy you are, and how much to be envied, if you are His seed in that also. To suffer injury and pain, and shame and humiliation at home and abroad, and never to retaliate, or to let it be seen that you suffer so acutely. Happy communicant! The seed and the solace of Christ if that is so! My brethren, almost above everything else in this world, imitate Christ in His silence. For "the tongue can no man tame." No man, but the Man of Sorrows. But He can. He tamed the tongue in Himself, and He is taming it in you, if you are indeed His seed. More and more imitate Him, then, amid all the injuries and insults, and provocations, and vexations, and even annoyances that are let loose upon you every day—and for this very end—that your Redeemer may see His seed in you and in your silence under injuries and wrongs. "For hereunto also are ye called."

"Neither was any deceit in His mouth." Now, cleanse your mouth also of all duplicity and double-mindedness. Be sincere and simple; and in everything and to every man be honest and honourable. Let your yea be yea, and your nay, nay. Till the God of all truth and all integrity shall see His true children in you, and till the Son of God shall see His true seed in you.

And to sum up: "He was numbered with the transgressors: and He bore the sin of many, and made intercession for the transgressors." This is the crowning grace of Christ, both in Messianic prophecy and in its evangelical fulfilment: "He made intercession for the transgressors," and especially for those who had transgressed against Himself. Do you the same! Shut your door, and do the same! Make intercession for those who will never know it till the books are opened, that you may be the children of your Father which is in heaven; and that Christ Jesus may be the Firstborn among many such brethren as you. "For as many as are led by the Spirit of God" in such things as these, "they are the sons of God. The Spirit also bearing witness with our Spirit, that we are the children of God. And, if children, then heirs, heirs of God, and joint heirs with Christ: if so be that we suffer with Him, that we may be also glorified together."

17

The Ransom

To give His life a ransom for many (Matt. 20:28).

Let us draw near this morning and join ourselves to our Lord when He is on His way up to the Passover for the last time. And let us abide near Him this morning till we see the end. And when we see the end, let us say for ourselves what Paul said for himself: "He loved me and gave Himself for me."

1. No sooner had our Lord entered Jerusalem in the beginning of that week than, in His own words, He began "to give His life a ransom." As long as His time had not yet come, our lord took great care of His life. His was the most precious life on the face of the earth, and He took corresponding care of it. But now that the work of His life was finished, He began at once to give His life away. All the beginning and middle of that Passover week our Lord was preaching all the daytime in the temple, and then at night He went out and abode in the Mount that is called the Mount of Olives. All that week, our Lord preached all day and prayed all night. Now there is nothing so exhausting as preaching unless it is praying—such preaching, that is, and such praying as our Lord's preaching and praying were all that Passover week. Paul in one place speaks about preaching the "terror of the Lord." And that terrible word best describes our Lord's last sermons in Jerusalem. It is remarkable, and there must be a good reason for it, that the only sermons of our Lord that we have anything like a full report of are His first sermon and His last—His sermon on the Mount and His three days of farewell sermons in the temple. That preacher was simply throwing his life away who delivered the discourses that Matthew has preserved in the end of his Gospel. He was walking straight into the jaws of death

who stood up in the temple, especially when there was not standing room in its Passover porches, and spoke the parable of "The Wicked Husbandman," and the parable of "The Marriage Feast," and the parable of "The Ten Virgins," and the parable of "The Last Judgment." And then, to make it impossible that His meaning could be missed, He hurled out such bolts of judgment as these: "Woe unto you, Scribes and Pharisees, hypocrites! Woe! Woe! Woe!" For three whole days the terrible Preacher was permitted to anticipate the Last Day; and no man laid hands on Him. And then, all night in the Mount of Olives, our Lord, all that week, was simply squandering away what remained of His life. Unless, indeed, He was in all that ransoming the lost lives of those preachers who tune their pulpits, and who, once they are home from their day's work and have well dined, will not venture out again after either to preach or to pray. The Son of Man gave His life for many ministers, in the temple and in the garden, as well as on the tree.

2. The calmness of mind and the careful deliberation with which our Lord goes about the Last Supper is very affecting and very impressive. The quiet and orderly way in which He gives his instructions about the Supper; the serene and stately way in which He performs His whole part in the Upper Room; the watchful solicitude He shows about the behaviour of the disciples both to Himself and to one another, while all the time His own terrible death was just at the door—it melts our hearts to see it all. He dwells on the Supper. He lingers over the Supper. He lengthens it out. He takes it up, part after part. He looks back at Moses in Egypt. He looks forward to the marriage supper of the Lamb. He legislates for the future of His ransomed Church and people. He takes the paschal lamb out of the Supper and He puts Himself in its place. "Take, eat, this is My body broken for you. This is My blood of the New Testament," said the Lamb of God, "shed for many for the remission of sins; drink ye all of it. And do this till I come." What a heart-melting sight! What nobleness! What peace! What beauty of holiness! What boundless love!

3. "Then cometh Jesus with them to a place called Gethsemane, and saith to the disciples, Sit ye there while I go and pray yonder."

Our Lord is in no mood for mockery, but our hearts read their own bitterness into His departing words. He seeks out a seat for the disciples. He seeks out the best, the softest, and the most sheltered seat in the garden. He points them to the place, and He bids them sit down in it. He tells them to keep near one another, and to keep one another company. And before He has got to His place "yonder," they are all fast asleep! *He* has not slept for a week. Night after night He has spent in that same spot, till even Judas "knew the place." More than the city watchmen for the morning He had waited for God in that garden all that week; and He still waits. "Out of the depths have I cried to Thee, O Lord. Out of the belly of hell, O Lord. Then I passed me about even to the soul; the weeds were wrapped about my head." And being in an agony, He prayed more earnestly; and His sweat was as it were great drops of blood falling to the ground. It was the wages of sin. It was the Lord laying on Him the iniquities of us all. It was—every ransomed soul knows what it was. "Yes; it was *my* cup," says every ransomed soul. "I mingled it; I filled it; I have sometimes just tasted it. No wonder He sweat blood as He drank it. For that cup was *sin*. It was the wages of my sin. It was full of the red wine of the wrath of God against me." And when He rose off His face and left the trampled-down and blood-soaked winepress, He found the disciples still sleeping. And again our hearts mock at us as He says, "Sleep on now, and take your rest."

4. Were you ever false as hell to your best friend? Did you ever take your unsuspecting friend by the hand and say, Welcome! or Farewell? Was there ever a sweet smile on your face, while there was a dagger under your cloak? Did envy, or ambition, or revenge, or some such pure and downright evil ever enter your heart, till you almost went out and hanged yourself with horror at yourself? Then thou art the man that Jesus Christ ransomed from the halter and from hell when He submitted His cheek to the kiss of the traitor. It is because Jesus Christ has you and so many like you among His disciples that He took so meekly the diabolical embrace of the son of perdition. "It was not an enemy that reproached me; then I could have borne it. Neither was it he that hated me that did magnify himself against me; then would I have hid myself from him. But it was thou, a man

mine equal, my guide and mine acquaintance. We took sweet counsel together, and walked into the house of God in company. Yea, mine own familiar friend, in whom I trusted, which did eat of my bread, hath lifted up his heel against me." "For we ourselves were sometimes living in malice and envy, hateful and hating one another. But after that the kindness and love of God our Saviour toward man appeared—not by works of righteousness which we have done, but according to His mercy He saved us, by the washing of regeneration and the renewing of the Holy Ghost, which He shed on us abundantly, through Jesus Christ our Saviour, that being justified by His grace, we should be made heirs according to the hope of eternal life."

5. "Then the band and the captain and the officers of the Jews took Jesus and bound Him." It is a very bitter moment to a prisoner when the officers of justice are binding him. I have often thought that the pinioning before execution must be almost more dreadful than the very drop itself. And our Lord felt most acutely the shame and the disgrace of the prison shackles. For once He broke silence and spoke out and remonstrated. "Be ye come out as against a thief?" He turned upon the officers. He had no intention of trying to escape. He had come out to the garden to give Himself up. He had said just the moment before, "I am He. Take Me, and let these go their way." But the officers were under the instructions of Judas. Their superiors in the city had told them that they were to look to Judas for all their orders that night. And Judas had said to the officers: "Whomsoever I shall kiss, that same is He; take Him and lead Him away safely; that same is He, hold Him fast." And they obeyed Judas; they held Him as fast and as safe as their best prison-cords could hold Him. O officers! Officers! Judas must surely know; but it is impossible that you can know why it is that your prisoner walks with you so willingly! Did any of you Roman officers ever hear of "cords of love?" Well, it is in the cords of everlasting love that you keep your man so safely tonight. O officers! Officers! If you only knew who that is you are leading in cords into the city! O Judas, Judas! What are thy thoughts? O! Better never to have been born!

6. "And all His disciples forsook Him and fled. But Peter followed Him afar off, unto the high priest's palace, and went in and sat with

the servants to see the end." Did you ever deny a friend? Did you ever sit still and hear a friend of yours slandered, witnessed against by hired witnesses, and condemned? Did you ever sit and warm yourself at some man's fire; or more likely, at some man's wine; and for fear, for cowardice, or for the sake of the company and the good cheer did you nod and smile and wink away your absent brother's good name? Look, redeemed dastard! Look at thy dreadful ransom! Look at Jesus Christ in the hard hands, and under the hired tongues of His assassins—and Peter, His sworn friend, washing his hands of all knowledge of the friendless Prisoner! Look! O dog in the shape of a man! All their sham charges, all their lying of witnesses, all their judicial insults and brutalities are clean forgotten by Peter's Master! He does not hear what they are saying, and He does not care. A loud voice out in the porch has stabbed our Lord's heart to death. "I know not the Man! I never saw Him till tonight!" With oaths and curses above all the babel, Peter's loud voice rolls in on his Master: "I know not the Man!" And the cock crew. And the Lord turned and looked upon Peter. And Peter went out and wept bitterly. And as the fine legend has it, Peter never heard a cock crow, day nor night, all his after days, that he did not remember the Passover porch of Caiaphas the High Priest that year in Jerusalem!

7. You have heard sometimes about hell being let loose. Yes, but hear this. Come to Caiaphas' palace on the Passover night and look at this. "Then did they spit in His face, and buffeted Him; they blindfolded Him and then they smote Him with the palms of their hands, saying: Prophesy to us, Thou Christ, who is it that smote Thee? And they stripped Him, and put on Him a scarlet robe. And when they had platted a crown of thorns"—I wonder in what sluggard's garden it grew!—"they put it upon His head, and a reed in His right hand; and they bowed the knee before Him and mocked Him, saying: Hail! King of the Jews! And they spit upon Him again, and took the reed out of His hand, and smote Him upon the head. Then Pilate took Jesus and scourged Him. After which they brought Jesus forth wearing the crown of thorns and the purple robe. And when the Chief Priests saw Jesus, they cried out, Crucify Him! crucify Him! Then Pilate delivered Him to them to be crucified." My brethren, these are

dreadful, most dreadful things. And all the time, God Almighty, the God and Father of Jesus Christ, restrained Himself; He held Himself in and sat as still as a stone, seeing and hearing all that. The arrest, the trial, the buffeting, the spitting, the jesting and the jeering, the bloody scourging, the crown of thorns, the reed, and the purple robe. Why? In the name of amazement, why did the Judge of all the earth sit still and see all that said and done? Do you know what made Him sit still? Did you ever think about it? And would you like to be told how it could be? God Almighty, my brethren, not only sat still, but He ordained it all; and His Son *endured* it all, *in order to take away sin*. In order to take away the *curse* of sin, to take away the very existence of sin for ever. You will find the explanation of that terrible night's work, and of the still more terrible morning just about to dawn. You will find the explanation, the justification, and the complete key to it all *in your own heart*.

Did you ever see yourself to be such a despicable creature that you wondered why all men did not spit upon you? Did you ever wonder that, not friendship and family life only, but very human society itself, did not dissolve and fall in pieces, such is the meanness, the despicableness, the duplicity, the selfishness, the cruelty, and the diabolical wickedness of the human heart—but above all human hearts, of yours? You will understand the spitting-scene that night when God lets you see your own heart. There was no surplus shame; there was no scorn too much; the contumely was not one iota overdone that night. There was no unnecessary disgrace poured on Christ that night. They are in every congregation, at every Communion Table, and they are the salt and the ornament of it, who say as they sit down at the Table: "He hid not His face from shame and from spitting for me! He loved me in my sin and my shame, and He gave Himself for me!"

8. If all that will not melt your heart of stone, try the next thing that Pilate and his devils did. For Pilate scourged Him. I will leave the scourging to yourselves to picture, and to ask, What is scourging? Who was it that was that morning scourged? And why was He scourged being innocent? And the crown of thorns, and all the awful scene to the end! O that mine head were waters and mine eyes a fountain of tears!

9. But come out to Calvary at nine o'clock that morning if you would be absolutely glutted with sorrow and with love. All the shame, all the scorn, all the horror, all the agony due to our sin, and undertaken by our Surety—it all met on the Cross. The Cross was the vilest, the cruellest, the most disgraceful, the most diabolical instrument of execution that ever hell had invented and set up on earth. Stand back and let the chiefest sinner in this house come forward. Give him the best place. Whoever sees the crucifixion, let *him* see it. Look, sinner, and see. They lay down the Cross on the ground. They then take the cords off our Lord's pinioned arms, and the painted board off His breast. They then lay Him down on His back on the Cross; they stretch out His arms along the arms of the Cross. They then open out His hands; and with a hammer they drive a great nail of iron through His right hand with the blood spurting up in their faces; and another through His left hand, and another through His feet, placed the one above the other to save the nails. Five or six strong soldiers then lift up the Cross with its trembling, bleeding Burden, and sink it down with a dash into the stone socket, set in the earth, till all His bones are out of joint. And "They know not what they do!" is all He says. No; *they* know not, but the chief of sinners now looking on, he knows. Paul knew. "He loved me," said Paul, "and gave Himself for me." Cowper knew.

> There is a fountain filled with blood
> Drawn from Immanuel's veins;
> And sinners, plunged beneath that flood,
> Lose all their guilty stains.

We often pray that God would "make the bed" of His dying saints, and He does it. But that was the deathbed God made for His dying Son!

But all that, after all, was but the outer porch of death to our Lord. Gethsemane and Caiaphas and Pilate and Herod's palace were but the outer court of the temple. The Cross was the altar; and the sacrifice only began to be fully offered about the sixth hour when there was darkness over all the earth till the ninth hour. It passeth all understanding, and all the power of tongue and pen, what the Son of

God suffered in body and in soul during those three dark and silent hours. Only at the ninth hour Jesus cried with a loud voice, "My God, My God: why hast Thou forsaken Me?" And some time after, "It is finished," when He bowed His head and gave up the ghost.

> 'Tis finished—was His latest voice:
> These sacred accents o'er
> He bowed His head, gave up the ghost,
> And suffered pain no more.
>
> 'Tis finished: The Messiah dies
> For sins, but not His own:
> The great redemption is complete
> And Satan's power o'erthrown.

"So, after He had taken His garments and was set down again, He said unto them: Know ye what I have done to you?"

Yea, Lord. Thou hast given Thy life a ransom for many. Thou hast loved me and given Thyself for me!

> I am not worthy, holy Lord,
> That Thou shouldst come to me;
> Speak but the word; one gracious word
> Can set the sinner free.
>
> I am not worthy; cold and bare
> The lodging of my soul;
> How canst Thou deign to enter there?
> Speak, Lord! and make me whole.
>
> I am not worthy; yet, my God,
> How can I say Thee nay—
> Thee, Who didst give Thy flesh and blood
> My ransom price to pay?
>
> O come, in this sweet morning hour
> Feed me with food Divine;
> And fill with all Thy love and power
> This worthless heart of mine.

18

Crucified with Christ

I am crucified with Christ: nevertheless I live; yet not I, but Christ liveth in me: and the life which I now live in the flesh I live by the faith of the Son of God, Who loved me, and gave Himself for me (Gal. 2:20).

What is this that Paul says: "I am crucified with Christ"? What does the Apostle really mean? In what sane and solid sense does he use these hitherto unheard-of words? Saul of Tarsus, we have his own word for it, had never seen Christ, nor His Cross either. He had not been in Gethsemane with Christ like Peter, nor on Calvary with Him like John. The two thieves might have said, "We were crucified with Christ," but how could Saul of Tarsus say it? For he was still at home in his own country; he was only as yet an aspirant to Gamaliel's school when Christ was crucified; and the crucifixion of Christ was long past before Saul had set a foot in the City of the Crucifixion. In what sense then can he say, and say it so often and so boldly, "I am crucified with Christ"? My brethren, he says it because he believes it. He says it because he has experienced it, and because he is sure of it, as sure of it as he is sure that he is alive. Paul was not only the greatest preacher of the Cross that ever lived; he was that because he was more than that, and better than that; for he was the greatest and best believer the doctrine of the Cross ever had. Peter and John might hesitate and hedge in preaching fully and freely the Cross of Christ, and all the doctrines of grace that depend upon it; they might dissemble and dissimulate for fear of them that were of the circumcision, but Paul never. He knew what he said, and he meant it down to the very bottom, all that he said. He said it; and he shook them that seemed to be pillars in Jerusalem by the way he said it. "I am crucified with Christ... and though an angel from heaven were to preach any other Gospel than the Gospel of a believing sinner's crucifixion with Christ, let him be accursed. For I certify you, brethren, that my Gospel is not after man. For I neither received it of man, neither was I taught it, but by revelation of Jesus Christ."

What, then, is this Gospel that Paul so immediately learned and so fully and so faithfully preached? What is the Gospel of the cross, and of a sinner's crucifixion with Christ upon the cross? No man need misunderstand or be ignorant of the Apostle's central doctrine if he wishes to understand it, and takes any trouble to understand it. For he makes it quite plain in every Epistle of his. He preaches nothing else. He has nothing else to preach. Another Gospel is not another. There is no other Gospel. It is to the cross Paul is leading up in all his teaching about the law of God, and about the nature and estate of man; and it is from the same cross he leads his readers down again when he writes of the new life, the peace, the joy, the strength, the blessedness of all those who, like himself, have been crucified with Christ. And all up and down his splendid Epistles he throws in those glorious glimpses of his own experiences which make all his Epistles so everyday-like and experimental, amid all their sweep and magnificence, and amid all their height and depth. The seventh of Romans, the third of Philippians, the whole of the Corinthians and the Galatians, are full of Christ and His cross; and, at the same time, they are full of Paul and his crucifixion with Christ and his consequent "life unto God." And in this text that autobiographic Gospel of Paul comes to its most condensed and most compacted expression.

Paul's first experience of the law of God was a terrible experience. He tells the tragical story to the Roman believers, to enforce upon them the necessity, sweetness, and blessedness of the cross. Like a fierce accuser, like a dreadful judge, like a deadly executioner the law of God all at once fell upon Paul, fell upon him and haled him to prison and death and judgment just as he had been wont to hale the disciples of Christ. But, behold, just as the executioner's axe was lifted up against Paul, God Himself interposed and said: "Save: I have found a ransom." "God," said Paul speaking of that time, "God revealed His Son in me," and revealed Him on His cross.

And though Christ had been crucified long before on Calvary, yet Paul saw Him "evidently set forth" during those three days in Damascus. For three days the mystery of the cross being opened to Paul; and I think it likely to certainty that Paul during those three days went down deeper into the mystery of Redemption than any mortal man had ever done before, or has ever done since. No man can come near that mystery and live; the man Christ Jesus died as He entered into it; and while Paul was having it revealed somewhat unto him he lay as good as dead. He was three days without sight, and did neither eat nor drink. But during those three dead days he had sights given him to see, and meat given him to eat, that the Damascus world around him knew not of. He was like those mysterious beings in heaven who are "full of eyes within"; and with his deep inward eyes Paul saw, as he lay at the mouth of hell—he saw, I say, that he was brought up from hell, and taken up into heaven, that he might fully and fearlessly preach. He saw Jesus Christ, the Son of God, upon the cross; and he saw Him there made sin for him, that he might be made the righteousness of God in Him. Nor did Paul merely see that cross and lie three days and three nights looking at it. No. Paul was more than a spectator and a student of the cross of Christ. Paul was lifted up upon the cross and was himself crucified with Christ. Whether in the body, or out of the body, Paul could never tell; but ere ever he was aware, he was lifted up and lost to law and life and all things upon that awful, that wondrous, that glorious cross. That last thing he remembered was his being lifted up upon that cross. He did not remember dying; he did not remember being dead. The last thing he remembered was, with an awful boldness, laying and leaving his conscience of sin on the thorn-crowned head of the crucified One. And in that dying act Paul's whole life—his guilt, his condemnation, his curse, his very existence—was all drunk up by that cross. Paul was as if he had never been born during those three terrible days. After those days were over there arose from the earth on which Paul had lain, there came down from the cross on which Paul was crucified, a man, a form of a man in some outward respect not unlike Paul; but it was not the former Paul at all. Those Damascus disciples he had come to persecute trembled when they saw Paul, as they thought, on their streets and in their synagogue, but there was no cause. The Paul they had heard of was dead, and his world would see him no more. He was dead, and his bones were scattered at the grave's mouth. So effectually, so completely, so utterly did Paul die on the cross with Christ. Now, do not delude yourselves and say that this was all an imagination, Paul's powerful and evangelical imagination. No. All this is as real as life and death are real; as law and justice, judgment and eternity, God and Christ are real. Paul's unreal and imagined life was when he was yet at Gamaliel's school, and on the road to Damascus. After he fell from his horse he came to himself; he became sane and wise for the first time; and this earth has never seen a saner, wiser, nobler man than Paul the Apostle who was crucified with Christ.

Only, let Luther utter a caution to us here. And let him utter his caution out of that book of which John Bunyan said that he preferred it before all the books he had ever seen as most fit for a wounded conscience. "Paul," says Luther, commenting on this very text, "Paul speaks not here of crucifying by imitation or example, for to follow the example of Christ is also to be crucified with Him. This crucifying is not that of which Peter speaks, that Christ left us an example that we should follow in his steps. But Paul speaketh here of that high crucifying, whereby sin, and the devil, and death are crucified in Christ, and not in me. Here Christ doth all Himself alone. But I, believing in Christ, am by faith also crucified with Christ, so that sin, and death, and the devil are all crucified and dead unto me." In Bunyan's day the books that taught this doctrine were like to fall to pieces if one did but turn them over! Such books were then the meat and drink of heroes; they were the consolation and the strength of saints.

"I am crucified with Christ; nevertheless I live." "This is a great mystery even to myself," says Paul, "but I will tell you how it has been fulfilled in me. When the law of God came home to me, I saw that I was a dead man. I saw that the wages of sin like mine was death. But just then it was that God in His grace to me revealed His Son in me. Revealed Him in me a very mystery of godliness; revealed Him as made sin, as crucified for sin, and thus as the ransom and redeemer of my soul. Had I died for my own sin, which I was just about to do, I had died the first and the second death. But dying in and with Christ, I both died and yet lived. One with Him in His death, I began again to live in His resurrection life. I awoke off and after the cross, and found myself a new creature; old things passed away, and all things had become new. I am still dead to some things—dead and never to see resurrection. I am dead to the law, and the law is dead to me. The law still sometimes looks at me as if it knew me, and had something against me, and was about to bring up something against me; but after a time it only looks at me and passes by me. At such moments I tremble to my very heart; but at such moments God again reveals His Son in me, and I am enabled to say: "Why art thou disquieted in me, O my soul? thou and I are crucified with Christ!"

"Nevertheless I live. I live, I say, yet I so live that it is not I that live, but rather it is Christ that liveth in me. In some ways I am the same man I was before I was crucified with Christ, and in some ways I am not. In some not unimportant ways I am the same man, and in some more important ways I am not. My hands and my feet are the same hands and feet I had before I was crucified with Christ; and yet even they are not quite the same, for they henceforth bear in them the marks of the Lord Jesus. The outward man is much the same; but the inward man has had a wonderful experience. I was a dead man, a mere corpse and carcass of a man, when the Lord Jesus came to me, and breathed His own life into me, and said unto me, Saul, Saul, receive thou the Holy Ghost! And I arose and stood upon my feet a living man. I lived, yet not I, but at that moment Christ lived in me."

The next clause is just a repetition, and explanation, and an expansion of what he has already said: "The life which I now live in the flesh I live by the faith of the Son of God." "The life which I now live in the flesh" just means this life you see me live among you, this life of Paul upon the earth, and among the churches, this life of continually travelling about, now east and now west, alternately preaching and tent-making, establishing Churches and writing Epistles. Beneath all that, and behind all that, there lies and works in me this great Gospel mystery of life and death, crucifixion and resurrection, justification and sanctification. I bear about with me daily, in doing all this, the dying of the Lord Jesus; and the life of Jesus is, at the same time, I trust, somewhat made manifest in my mortal body. For this life I now live in the flesh and on the earth, and till I go to be with Christ which is far better—this present life I live by faith in the Son of God. My life is not led in obedience to the law; the law and I are for ever done with one another. I have said in every Epistle of mine that I am dead to the law; and in this matter I do not write one thing and live another. I do not build again the things I destroyed. Let this be known then as the first article of my creed, and not more my creed than my practice. I, Paul, am dead to the law, and the law to me. So much so that even where I seem to you to obey and not to break the law, it is not the law I obey at all, for I am dead to it. If obedience to the law comes about by my faith in Christ, good and well. But the law I am under, and the law I obey, is the law and life of Jesus Christ. Holiness itself, complete and spotless holiness, would not win me back to the law, or reconcile me to its dominion, or authority, or rewards. I would not have holiness and eternal life by the law even if it were offered me. I have suffered too much from the law ever again to trust it; no law for me any more! Christ, and Christ alone, is lawgiver and righteousness, power and truth, strength and salvation, temporal and eternal life to me! He is "made of God to me wisdom, and righteousness, and sanctification, and redemption." I am complete in Him, and the law will never more find me among its disciples, its devotees, or its debtors. For I, through the law, am dead to the law, that I might live unto God! Unto God, by faith in His Son. His Son, I say, Who loved me and gave Himself for me.

The law never loved me nor gave a hair of its head for me. Even when I obeyed it above many my equals in my own nation, all the time it never loved me. And then, when I, in its least commandment, inadvertently and unconsciously broke it, it turned upon me with its bowels of brass and its flaming sword. But O, the depth of the grace of God! I see now that the Son of God loved me even when I was dead in trespasses and sins; and I now love Him because He first loved me. And if you speak of commandments and of obedience and of the law, I will keep all His commandments and all His law, and obey Him, because He first loved me and gave Himself for me. I love

Him now, and He knows it; but He loved me first. He was beforehand with His love. It was His part and privilege to love me first. He was the Son and He loved me, and revealed to me the age and the depth and the strength of His love, and by all that He carried my heart captive, and keeps it captive in a willing, a holy, and an everlasting captivity. Me! Ay, me! "Me—He loved me," says Paul. Paul does not grudge or deny or forget the love of Christ to Peter, or James, or John, or the Galatian believers. At another time he will write to them about that, and will powerfully commend the love of Christ to their hearts; but what he has before him today is this: that Christ loved him, loved Paul himself—yes, Paul himself. For the time Paul takes the whole of Christ's love to himself, the whole of Christ's heart, the whole of His cross, the whole of His atoning death, the whole of His blood, and the whole of His righteousness.

"He loved me and gave Himself for me." Paul is back again in a moment at the cross of Christ. The mere mention of Christ's love to Paul brings back the thought of his sin with a rush of darkness upon his heart, and a rush of blood to his cheek; and before he can finish the verse, he has to go back to the cross of Christ and finish it there. He gave Himself for me, says Paul—for me and for my sins. Not for sin, not for the sin of the world, but for the sin of Paul. For the sin that made Paul all his days the chief of sinners, and kept him all his days the least of all saints; for that sin that was the thorn of Satan in his flesh, and the sword of God in his bones, and the sting of death as often as he thought of death—for me and for my sins. And then this great verse returns upon itself, returns upon the cross, and is locked into a golden chain of salvation, holding Christ and Paul in one bundle of life for ever: one cross, one crucifixion, one blood, one righteousness, one death, one life, one Father, and one everlasting home with Him. "I am crucified with Christ… who loved me, and gave Himself for me."

Now, what bearing has all this on our circumstances and prospects here today? Much bearing, my brethren—in many ways, and in this way. For one thing, the law will be sure to cross over and intrude itself into the province of grace this day. The law will thrust itself into many an evil conscience this day. It will stand with its flaming sword at the door of the table today and will say to some of you: What dost thou here? Thou art a sinner. What hast thou to do to take God's covenant into thy mouth? Take care, it will say, lest God strike thee dead while yet the cup is in thy unclean hand! What dost thou here, thou chief of sinners? And it will fling in thy face some of thy worst sins and will defy thee to come to the table.

Now what, in that case, are you to do? Do you know what to do? Hast thou learned of Paul what to do at such a solemn moment? I will tell thee what to do. Have thy New Testament open at this text. Place thy finger upon this text, and take heart and say: All thou sayest about me, O accusing law, is all true. But I come here this day on another title and token than thou canst either give me or take away from me. I come here into His house on the token and invitation and command of Jesus Christ. I come because He said: "If ye love Me, this do in remembrance of Me." And I will not go back till He turns me back Himself. Nay, though He seemed to turn me back, I would not believe my eyes. Though He said, "Friend, how camest thou hither?" Though He said, "Let the children first be filled." And even though He said, "Bind him hand and foot"—while they so bind me I will still say: "Just and true are Thy ways, thou King of Saints; but Thou knowest all things, and thou knowest that I love Thee!" Say that; I have told thee what to say.

19

To the Uttermost

Able to save to the uttermost (Heb. 7:25).

"The uttermost" is the strongest and the extremest word in all the world. There cannot be anything beyond the uttermost. The uttermost is situated on the very extremest rim, and on the very outmost edge, of all existing things. All existence absolutely ends and comes to its everlasting limit when it comes to its uttermost. Beyond the uttermost, blank annihilation and sheer nothingness alone exist. We may labour the thought, and we may repeat and multiply the word till we are wearied; but after we have done all, we must always end with this: that the uttermost is just the uttermost; and beyond the uttermost neither the experience of man can pass, nor the imagination of man can picture.

Now, as there is something that is the very uttermost in the world of time, and as there is something that is the very uttermost in the world of space, so there is something that is the very uttermost in the world of sin and in the world of salvation. It is not given to any mortal man to know when the uttermost moment of time is to come. "Of that day, and that hour, knoweth no man: no, not the angels which are in heaven; neither the Son, but the Father." And as for the uttermost point of space, some men of science are so perplexed with it as to think that space must be absolutely infinite, like its maker.

And no more does any man know what is the uttermost limit of sin and misery. Who is the uttermost of all sinners? Who can tell? But that there is such a sinner somewhere, still sinning on earth, or saved in heaven, or suffering in hell; and that Almighty God knows that sinner, and knows all about him; all that is quite certain. There is something in that sinner's case, there has been something in that sinner's career, that conclusively stamps him as the very uttermost of all sinners anywhere to be found. In God's sight, and in God's judgment, there is some sinner somewhere who bears away the palm.

"All have sinned and come short of the glory of God." But there are great differences in the length to which sinners have gone in their sins. "All sins are in all," said the Stoics; "but all sins have not come to the light in all." There is no sin so sinful but that any sinner might have committed it. At the same time, and as a matter of fact, some sinners far outstrip other sinners, and leave them quite out of sight. "Are all transgressions of the law equally heinous?" No. By no means. "Some sins in themselves, and by reason of several aggravations, are more heinous in the sight of God than others." Now, it is the "aggravations" of our sins that carry us away past all other sinners, and make us the very uttermost of all sinners. And thus it is that the uttermost sinner is not at all to be looked for where we would first think of looking for him. We speak of Christendom and of heathendom. And we would naturally look for the chief of sinners among the nations that know not God. But he is not to be found where we would naturally look for him. Not at all. "Circumstances," says a great experimental preacher, "lie far heavier on the soul than the sin itself." And the circumstances of a sinner in a Christian land lie far heavier on his conscience, and stand far blacker against him in the book of judgment, than if he had lived and died in a heathen land. This is how a deeply exercised saint used to examine himself as to the circumstances and the aggravations of his sins. "My age," he used to say, "and my office? My place of love, and honour, and trust, in the family, and in the Church? The time and the occasion of my sin? The true name of my sin, if it were to be proclaimed from the housetop? The contempt and the defiance of God revealed in my sin? Done once only? or done often? and done presumptuously, and done insultingly, and after frequent forgiveness?" And so on, through a whole world of circumstances and aggravations. Yes, it is the circumstances and the accompaniments of sin that so blacken the book of God, and so exasperate and horrify the awakened conscience of the sinner.

And thus it is that the very uttermost sinner in all this city this morning is to be looked for in some of its congregations, rather than in any of its slums or in any of its prisons. Those outcast creatures that fill our sunken places, our prisons, and our penal settlements, may well have committed crimes that we have never had any temptation to commit. But by no possibility can they be guilty of such sins, and such heinous aggravations of sins, as some of us are guilty of. They never had the thousandth part of our advantages and opportunities. And it is advantage and opportunity that so aggravate sin, and so incriminate the soul. I should not wonder then that the very uttermost sinner in all this city this morning is sitting in this house at this moment, and is consenting to my words about him with his whole heart. It is quite possible, and there are some good grounds for believing it, that there is some man here on whom privilege upon privilege has been heaped, and opportunity upon opportunity, and grace upon grace, and all conceivable kinds of blessing—both temporal and spiritual—and yet he has sinned in the teeth of all that till he is the very uttermost sinner in all this city. And till it may very well be that what is so much mere hypothesis, and imagination, and indeed extravagance, to all other men now listening to his case, is the most undeniable truth, and the most dreadful truth to him. Ay, and it may very well be that, under the hand of the Holy Ghost, he may be seeing at this moment how near he now is to the last precipice of all, how near he now is to that black line of reprobation beyond which there is nothing but the bottomless pit. But he is still here. He has not yet crossed the black line. He has not yet fallen headlong into that horrible pit. "Save from going down to the pit! For I have found a ransom." "Bring forth the best robe, and put it on him. For this my son was dead, and is alive again; he was lost, and is found!"

But that is not all. Would God it were all. But it is not all, by a long way. For, over and above the outward world of actual and aggravated sin, there is the far more awful world of secret sinfulness, a whole world of inward wickedness that far surpasses all our powers of self-examination. And here, also, there must be some saint of God, somewhere, either in grace or in glory, either on earth or in heaven, who had, or who has, in himself, the very uttermost of "indwelling sin." Who, I wonder, was he? Or, if he is now alive, who is he? Was it David, who was wont to cry that there was "no rest in his bones because of his sin"? And again, that his "loins were filled with a loathsome disease"? And again, that he was "shapen in iniquity"? Or was it Isaiah? "Woe is me, for I am undone!" Or was it Daniel when his "comeliness was turned to corruption"? Or was it the Apostle Paul, whose seventh chapter is such an outburst of unparalleled agony? Or was it Luther? "When a man like me," says the Reformer, "comes to know the plague of his own heart, he is not miserable only, he is absolute misery itself." Or was it Samuel Rutherford, who used to say: "When I look at the sinfulness of my own heart, my salvation is to me my Saviour's greatest miracle. He has accomplished nothing like my salvation"? Or was it Jacob Behmen, the uttermost of God's unsanctified saints, when he wrote: "Do not mistake me, for my heart is as full of malice sometimes as it can hold"? "Begone!" shouted Philip Neri to those who spoke to his praise. "Begone! for I am good for nothing but to think and to do evil!" "I am made of sin," sobbed Bishop Andrewes, till his private prayer book was all but undecipherable to his literary executors because of its author's sweat and tears. "It has often appeared to me," said the seraphic Jonathan Edwards, "that if God were to mark my heart iniquity against me, my bed would be in hell." But time would fail me to tell you the half of the agonising cries that I hear going up to heaven from the utmost corner of the land.

Now, which of all these was the "uttermost" sufferer because of his indwelling sin. Who shall say? Or whether it was any of those sufferers, or whether that greatest sufferer may not be some one of ourselves. Who can tell? It is quite possible; and the day will declare. For "the secret of the Lord is with them that fear Him; and He will show them His holy covenant."

We cannot be absolutely sure till we see them with our own eyes in heaven; but I think I am quite safe in saying that their Saviour has saved all those great sinners by this time, and that to "the uttermost." He has saved them from the uttermost of actual sin, and of indwelling sinfulness, and to the uttermost of holiness and of blessedness. I say, "the uttermost of holiness and of blessedness." For it is only those who have known in themselves the very "uttermost" of actual and indwelling sin, and all the shame and all the pain of it, who can by any possibility attain to the "uttermost" possession and enjoyment of true holiness, and the full blessedness of heaven. And there is a real fitness and fairness in that. "Blessed are they which do hunger and thirst after righteousness, for they shall be filled." And again: "Him that overcometh will I make a pillar in the temple of My God, and he shall go no more out. And I will write upon him the name of My God, and the name of the city of My God; and I will write upon him My new name."

The builder of a temple, who spares no expense, will sometimes bring his pillars from the very ends of the earth. Wherever he hears of a rock with rich enough veins of colour in it, and which is, at the same time, capable of taking on the finest finish, which is able to bear all his carving tools, and to receive all his intended polish and resplendence—with them rear a long vista of such pillars; till his temple is a perfect vision and a praise of all kinds of beauty. And something like that, says "He that is holy, He that is true," will it be in the heavenly temple. It is not by any means any and every stone that will take on all that is in the master-builder's mind. It is not every pillar that will carry all His Father's name, and all His own new name. And thus it is that wherever the Heavenly Builder finds such a possible "pillar," even if it is in the "utmost corner of the land," at any price He will purchase it for His great design, and will not leave off working on it, till He has set it, and in its proper place, in His heavenly temple.

And then, when, at the end of this world, that heavenly temple is at last finished—what a vision of strength and of beauty it will be! And supported and adorned with what a forest of dear-bought and far-borne pillars! And every pillar of them all written all over with the Builder's new name, and with His Father's name.

But, "What is His name, and what is His Son's name?" if thou canst tell. Yes, I can tell, and I will tell you. For, when a Gospel preacher is in the Spirit on the Lord's Day, a door is opened to him in heaven, and he is carried up to see the temple of God, and all its pillars, till he is able to tell, to all who have ears to hear, what is to be written on all the living pillars of that living temple. "Merciful," will be one of God's names written in letters of gold on many pillars.

"Gracious," in like letters on many other pillars. "Long-suffering," upon some; and "abundant in goodness and in truth," upon some. "He brought me up also out of an horrible pit, out of the miry clay," will shine on one great pillar; and on another, "Out of the belly of hell cried I, and He heard my voice." And on a pillar of the rarest beauty and perfection of form, this: "O wretched man that I was! But I thank God through Jesus Christ my Lord." Now what will be written upon you? For my part, you will read all these Scriptures written in large letters upon me. All these, and many more names of my God than all these. But especially, my text of this morning will be written upon me: "Saved to the uttermost!" Saved to the uttermost! And to go no more out! The Chief of Sinners, and saved to the uttermost.

"Now unto Him that is able to do exceeding abundantly above all that we ask or think, according to the power that worketh in us: unto Him be glory in the Church by Christ Jesus throughout all ages, world without end. Amen."

20

The New Wine of the Kingdom

I say unto you, I will not drink henceforth of this fruit of the vine, until that day when I drink it new with you in My Father's kingdom (Matt. 26:29).

Milton makes the angel say to Adam:

> What if earth
> Be but the shadow of heaven; and things therein
> Each to other like, more than on earth is thought?

That is to say: as the Passover Supper in Israel was but the "shadow" of the Lord's Supper in New Testament times, even so the Lord's Supper itself is but the "shadow" of the Marriage Supper of the Lamb. Butler also says, in his own deep and suggestive way, that "we are at present in the middle of a great progressive scheme of things, in the everlasting issues of which we are concerned far beyond all conception of ours." That is to say: the Lord's Supper is but one step in a great progressive scheme of evangelical things, of which we, at present, see next to nothing of their perfected end. And thus it is that this text, as it falls from our Lord's lips, carries the Lord's Supper away out of this present world of things altogether, and carries it away up into the new heavens and the new earth. The Lord's Supper, as we now celebrate it, has a great historical and commemorative significance. But it has a great prophetic and anticipative aspect also, in that it so plainly, and so impressively, points forward to the Marriage Supper of the Lamb. Let us take the Lord's Supper, then, as it is spread before us this morning, as the earthly "shadow" of the heavenly Supper. Let us look on our greatest means of grace on earth as, after all, but the sacramental pledge and foretaste of the far better things that God is preparing for them that love Him.

To begin at the beginning: What was Moses and his paschal lamb but the "shadow," not so much of the Lord's Supper on earth as of His far better Supper in heaven? The Old Testament lamb of Moses was the type of the New Testament Lamb of God. But for the once that our sin-atoning Lord is called "The Lamb of God" in the Gospel, He is called by that same atonement-name, actually, twenty-nine times in the Revelation. Now this continual remembrance of that atonement name of His in heaven is not without a great lesson to us, surely. That continually recurring name of His in heaven is surely intended to teach us that we shall see "the Lamb of God" in heaven, "as He was slain" on earth; and that we shall see Him then, with far more wonder, and far more praise than we can possibly see Him now. So true is it, and so true will it then be seen to be that this earth, at its best, is "but the shadow of heaven; and things therein each to other like, more than on earth is thought."

But to come down to our own day. Did you ever think, as you enjoyed them beyond all words, that all our communion seasons on earth are but so many shadows of the innumerable communion seasons that will come round to us in heaven? Sweet and sanctifying as they are, our very best communion seasons are not yet the Marriage Supper of the Lamb. At their best, our returning communion seasons are but the Betrothal Suppers of the Lamb. But in His Father's house in heaven, there will be a real and true Marriage Supper; when our too-long betrothal will, at last, be "fulfilled"—to use the Bridegroom's own glad word about it. Yes; and as those communion seasons, so to call them, come round in that world of things where time shall be no longer, but where there shall be something in the place of time—something that it hath not entered in the mind of man to imagine in the revolving years, so to call them, of the life everlasting—there will, no doubt, be seasons when all our past, both on earth and in heaven, will be called to remembrance, and will be sealed down anew upon our souls. And as we have "silver weddings" and "golden weddings" and "diamond weddings" on earth, in which we joyfully commemorate our happiest and our longest-lived weddings, even so there will be days of silver, and days of gold, and days of diamond in heaven, on which all the electing love of the Father, and all the redeeming love of the Son, and all the indwelling love of the Holy Ghost, will, again and again, be commemorated, and that in a way far more than a merely sacramental way. For then, a far

> …higher gift than grace
> Shall flesh and blood refine:
> Christ's Presence, and His very Self,
> And Essence all-Divine.

And then, for my part—do not be afraid or offended—I fully expect to enjoy not communion Sabbaths only in heaven, but fast days as well. Not fast days, indeed, when we shall hang our heads like a bullrush, and spread sackcloth and ashes under us. But fast days—so to call them—that shall be wholly fit for heaven, and entirely appropriate to heaven. We shall not indeed "examine ourselves" in heaven, as to our broken vows since last communion. But we shall sit apart for a season, watching with our Lord for "one hour," and shall examine ourselves as to our growth in glory, and in our ever-increasing likeness to Christ. There will be days in which we shall ask ourselves as to whether we are keeping sufficiently in mind the hole of the pit out of which we were dug. As also, if we are continually recollecting all else that God, in Christ, has done for our souls. And I quite anticipate that, at such seasons of self-examination, there will be some among us who will have a certain sadness in our souls as we call to mind the communion seasons of earth, and recollect how little we really examined and condemned ourselves on our appointed days of repentance, and with how little true preparation we ventured unto the Table. And all that will make us hasten to put on again the wedding garment of our Lord's imputed righteousness, clothed and adorned with which we shall again sit down at His table, and with this never-to-be-forgotten Psalm in our mouth:

> With us He dealt not as we sinned,
> Nor did requite our ill.

"Where wilt Thou," said Peter and John, "that we prepare for Thee to eat the Passover?" And He said unto them: "Behold, when ye have entered into the city, ye shall find a large upper room furnished: there make ready." And the two disciples did as they were commanded.

And they took the blood of the paschal lamb in a basin, and they struck it on the two side-posts, and on the upper doorpost of the house in which they were to eat the Passover. And the blood was a token upon that house all that night, until the morning. Peter and John were, in that way, our Lord's forerunners that Passover night in Jerusalem. But our Lord is our forerunner Himself in preparing for us to eat our true Passover Supper in the New Jerusalem. Indeed, our Lord bears in heaven that very name. "The Forerunner," says the Apostle, "even Jesus, is for us entered. By His own blood He hath for us entered into the Holy Place"—even as He said: "I go to prepare a place for you." "Now," says an old preacher on this point, "a forerunner is always a forerunner of followers, and of such followers as stay not long behind. And our Lord bears that excellent name because He has gone on before us to take up a place for us in His Father's House of many mansions. Earthly forerunners," that old preacher proceeds, "are wont to write the names of those who are to follow them, sometimes with chalk, and sometimes with paint, on the doors of the allotted lodgings; but we have such a 'forerunner' that He writes our names on the doorposts of heaven with His own blood. The sprinkled blood of the paschal lamb signed and sealed the identity and the ownership and the safety of every true Israelite's house in the land of Egypt. But all that was only an earthly 'shadow' of our far better signed and sealed lintel and doorpost in the new heaven and the new earth."

"And Jesus took bread, and blessed it, and brake it, and gave it to His disciples, and said to them: Take, eat: this is My Body broken for you. And He took the cup and gave thanks, and gave it to them, saying: Drink ye all of it." The Reformed Church finds two sacraments in Holy Scripture; while the Church of Rome finds seven in the Scriptures and in Church tradition. But the Church of Christ in Glory will have a whole multitude of sacraments. Indeed, there will be nothing to be seen, or tasted, or touched in heaven that will not be a true and fruitful sacrament.

For, "What is a Sacrament?" "A Sacrament is an holy ordinance instituted by Christ, wherein, by sensible signs, Christ and the benefits of the new covenant are represented, sealed, and applied to believers." And the whole of our Father's house, and of our own mansions in our Father's house, will be as full as they can hold of such sensible signs, so far as our senses will hold there, and will have their objects there. In this respect, it will be with us in heaven as it was with our Lord on earth. Everything He saw, as He went about, was a sacrament to Him. That is to say, everything He saw around Him represented, and sealed, and applied the new covenant and all its benefits, to Him and to His disciples. Did He, in one of His walks abroad, see a husbandman sowing seed in his field? So is the Kingdom of heaven, He said to Himself, and to His disciples. Did He see a vineyard, or a barren fig tree, or a lost sheep, or a piece of leaven, or a marriage supper, or a friend out at midnight to borrow loaves? Absolutely everything that our Lord saw on earth, in one way or other, spoke to Him something more concerning the Kingdom of heaven. And the same sacramental, that is to say, the same spiritual and imaginative mind, will by that time be found in all of us who shall be counted worthy communicants at the Table above. "Praise Him," we shall all sing with the Psalmist. "Praise Him, all ye His angels; praise Him, all ye His hosts. Praise Him, sun and moon; and all ye stars of light... mountains, and all hills; fruitful trees, and all cedars; beasts, and all cattle; creeping things, and flying fowl... both young men, and maidens; old men, and children... Praise Him with the sound of the trumpet. Praise Him with the psaltery and the harp. Praise Him with the timbrel, and in the dance. Praise Him with stringed instruments, and with organs. Yea, let everything that hath breath all unite to praise the Lord." So sacramental will the whole of creation have become to us all by that time. But most of all, the glorified Soul and the glorified Body of our Redeemer, with the sacramental marks of our redemption remaining on His hands, and on His feet, and on His side. "It was a wise design of Mark Antony," says Jeremy Taylor, "when he would stir up the people to revenge the death of Caesar: he brought the dead body to the pleading-place, and showed to all men his deadly wounds. He held up Caesar's stabbed mantle: the very mantle he put on that night in which he beat the Nervii. He put his finger in that fatal wound through which the dagger had pierced Caesar's heart. And he told them with what a love that heart had always loved them: so much so, that he had made the people of Rome the heirs of all his glory, and all his wealth, and had left to them so many places of delight and pleasure. And then, it was but natural that their grief at the loss of so honourable and so loved a lord should fill the people with a great sorrow and a great revenge."

And in like manner, there will be pleading-days and pleading-places in heaven where we shall see the "Lamb as He had been slain"; and where we shall be filled, as never before, with a great sorrow, and a great revenge, and an ever greater love. Yea, with what indignation; yea, with what fear; yea, with what vehement desire; yea, with what zeal; yea, with what revenge shall all our hearts be filled full! Till our full hearts shall again find vent in this commemoration psalm:

"Unto Him that loved us, and washed us from all our sins in His own blood; to Him be glory and dominion and power, for ever and ever. Amen!"

"But I say unto you, I will not henceforth drink of this fruit of the vine, until that day when I shall drink it new with you in My Father's Kingdom." I will drink wine new with you. That is to say—wine of a new kind. Wine out of a new vineyard. Wine out of a new winepress. Wine of a new sweetness, and new strength, and a new exhilaration. The fruit of the True Vine is love, joy, peace, gentleness, and all kinds of goodness; but, especially, love.

"Thy love is better than wine," the Bride shall say to the Bridegroom, as she leans on His breast at their marriage supper. And the Bridegroom shall answer her: "I am come into my garden, my sister, my spouse: I have gathered my myrrh with my spice: I have drunk my wine with my milk: eat, O Friends: drink, yea, drink abundantly, O Beloved." "This is my Beloved," shall the Bride then boast to all the daughters of Jerusalem. "This is my Beloved, and this is my Friend!" For I am my Beloved's, and He is mine! Yea, I am His, and He is mine!

Yes!—O Angel!

> What if earth
> Be but the shadow of heaven; and things therein
> Each to other like, more than on earth is thought!

PART FOUR
Last Messages

21

A Study in the Swelling of Jordan

How wilt thou do in the swelling of Jordan? (Jer. 12:5).

Both in its disputed rise, and in its zigzag course, and then in its inscrutable fall, the Jordan is the most wonderful, and indeed, in some respects, the most mysterious river on the face of the earth. Rising among the obscure rocks and tangled forests of the Lebanon, the Jordan rushes down through a deep and tortuous gorge that has seldom seen a bridge, and that only here and there has admitted a ford of the foot of man or beast. Walled in by high and overhanging rocks, the Jordan runs its crooked and angry course for some two hundred miles, till it loses itself in the Salt Sea, the Dead Sea of Sodom and Gomorrah. It was the absolutely miraculous passage of the Jordan by Joshua and the priests and the people of Israel that gave the Jordan such a place of wonder and of praise in the prophets and psalmists of Israel. And as time went on, the passage of the Jordan became a proverb and a prophecy of the passing of the immortal soul, out of this life of bitter bondage and of long and sore pilgrimage, into the Promised Land, the Promised Land of our Heavenly Father's house. And then, the prophet's solemnising challenge: *"How will thou do in the swelling of Jordan?"* That has come powerfully home to every man who has an evil conscience, and who has it before him to die and to go to judgment.

Well, then, before we come to *ourselves*, let us take a few moments to look at how some of our forerunners did when *they* came to the swelling of *their* "Jordan." And first, let us look at our blessed Lord Himself when He was approaching the dark river of death. For though He had no sin of His own to burden His conscience and to darken His heart, yet, at the same time, he was made such a surety and such a substitute for sinners that the swelling of His Jordan became an agony and indeed a terror to Him. So much so that even the pen of inspiration trembles to describe His dying experiences. Listen, then, with all the holy fear you can command, to what is tremblingly written concerning even the "Jordan" of our sinless Lord. "Now is My soul troubled; and what shall I say? Father, save Me from this hour." "Then took He with Him Peter and the two sons of Zebedee, and began to be sorrowful, and very heavy. Then saith He unto them, 'My soul is exceeding sorrowful, even unto death: tarry ye here, and watch with Me.' And then He went a little farther, and fell on His face, and prayed, saying: 'O My Father, if it be possible, let this cup pass from Me: nevertheless not as I will, but as Thou wilt.'" As Mark has it: "He began to be sore amazed, and to be very heavy." And as Luke has it: "Being in agony, He prayed more earnestly: and His sweat was as it were great drops of blood falling to the ground. And on the morrow, when it was about the sixth hour, there was a great darkness over all the land until the ninth hour. And the sun was darkened; and the veil of the temple was rent in the midst. And when He had received the vinegar, Jesus cried with a loud voice and said, 'Father! into Thy hands I commend My spirit!' And, having said this, He gave up the ghost." Now that, my brethren, was somewhat of how our Lord did in the swelling of *His* Jordan.

"And one of the malefactors which were crucified beside Him railed on Him, and said, 'If Thou be Christ save Thyself and us.' But the other answering rebuked him, saying, 'Dost thou not fear God, seeing thou art in the same condemnation? And we indeed justly; for we receive the due reward of our deeds: but this man hath done nothing amiss.' And he said unto Jesus, 'Lord remember me when Thou comest into Thy Kingdom.' And Jesus said to him, 'Verily I say unto thee, Today thou shalt be with Me in Paradise.'" And that was how the penitent thief did in swelling of *his* Jordan.

And *this* is how Stephen, the martyr-deacon, did. After he had spoken his great speech, his enemies were cut to the heart, and they rose upon him with one accord, and cast him out of the city, and stoned him to death; and he died calling upon God, and saying: "Lord Jesus, receive my spirit, and lay not this sin to their charge."

And they laid down their clothes at a young man's feet, whose name was Saul. And thirty years after that, Saul, by that time called Paul, descended into *his* Jordan with these words: "I thank Christ Jesus our Lord for putting me into the ministry; me, who was before a blasphemer and a persecutor; but I obtained mercy, that in me Jesus Christ might show forth all His long-suffering for a pattern to them which should hereafter believe on Him to life everlasting. And now, I am ready to be offered, and the time of my departure is at hand. And henceforth there is laid up for me a crown of righteousness, which the Lord, the righteous Judge, shall give me at that day; and not to me only, but unto all them also that love His appearing."

When Augustine saw that the swelling of *his* Jordan was fast approaching him, he got one of his divinity students to paint the thirty-second Psalm on the wall opposite his bed. And that great saint descended into his dark river, singing and saying:

> O blessed is the man to whom
> Is freely pardoned
> All the transgressions he hath done,
> Whose sin is covered.
> I will confess unto the Lord
> My trespasses, said I;
> And of my sin Thou freely didst
> Forgive the iniquity.

"Venerable Father," said Justus Jonas to Luther, when *he* was nearing *his* dark river: "Venerable Father, do you die trusting in Jesus Christ as your God and Saviour, and subscribing to the whole reformed doctrines that you constantly preached to us?" "Yes, certainly!" shouted the great Reformer with his last breath. "Yes, certainly! Jesus Christ is my Lord and my God, and He is my alone Righteousness and Strength both in death as in life!"

But by far and away our best handbook and guide-book as we draw near the swelling of *our* Jordan is John Bunyan's marvellous narrative of the various experiences of his puritan pilgrims, as they approached the dark river, and went through it. "Now, I further saw that betwixt them and the gate above was a river; but there was no bridge over the river; and the river was very deep. Then they addressed themselves to the water; and, entering, Christian began to sink, till he cried out to Hopeful, his neighbour, 'I sink in deep waters, the billows go over my head: all His angry waves go over me.' But Hopeful said, 'Be of good cheer, My Brother, for I feel the bottom; and it is good.' And with that Christian broke out with a loud voice, 'O! I see Him again! and He says to me, When thou passest through the waters, I will be with thee: and through the rivers, they shall not overflow thee.'"

And some time afterwards, when Christiana, the widow of Christian the pilgrim, came within sight of the same river, she called for Mr. Greatheart, her guide, and told him how matters stood with her. So he answered her, that he was heartily glad for her sake, and that he could have been glad had the heavenly post come for him. Then she called for her children; and what she said to them is all to be read at the end of her fine history. The last words she was heard to say here, were these: "I come, Lord, to be with Thee, and to bless Thee."

The next of that pilgrim company to come to the River was Mr. Ready-To-Halt. And the last words he was heard to say were these: "Welcome life." So he also went on his way.

After this, the same post sounded his horn at the chamber door of Mr. Feeble-Mind. And his last words were: "Hold out, Faith and Patience!" And saying so, he also went over to the other side.

How Mr. Despondency and his daughter Miss Much-Afraid got over, and what they said, I leave you to read for your own desponding and much-afraid selves.

As also dear old Honest, and his last words. And Mr. Valiant-For-Truth, and his brave words about his sword, and about his marks and his scars that he carried over with him. And to crown all, the magnificent speech of Mr. Standfast, than which even John Bunyan never penned two nobler pages. But how glorious it was to see how the regions beyond the dark river were all filled with horses and chariots; with pipers and with trumpeters; with singers with the voice and with players on stringed instruments; and all to welcome the pilgrims as they went up and followed one another in at the Beautiful Gate of the City! But among all John Bunyan's characters and their end, do not forget Mr. Fearing, who is in some respects the Tinker's spiritual and literary masterpiece.

A Study in the Swelling of Jordan

And now, after all that, I will only take time to give you Bishop Butler and *his* Jordan. When the great moralist, the old Honest of the Episcopal Bench, was on his deathbed, he called for his chaplain and said to him: "Though I have endeavoured to avoid sin, and to please God to the utmost of my power; yet from the consciousness of perpetual infirmities, I am still afraid to die." "My lord," said the chaplain, "you have forgotten that Jesus Christ is a Saviour." "True," said Butler, "but how shall I know that He is a Saviour for *me*?" "My lord, it is written, Him that cometh unto Me, I will in no wise cast out." "True," said the bishop; "and I am surprised a thousand times over, I never felt its virtue till this moment. And now I die happy."

Now, my brethren, let it be well understood and believed that all these dying men—from Jesus Christ Himself downward—were all but so many pioneers and forerunners to teach us how *we* are to do when we come to the swelling of our Jordan. And first, let us learn some much-needed lessons from our Lord Himself. And especially, *this* great lesson: to say at every step of our approach to our Jordan, and at every soul-sinking billow of it, "Thy will be done!" Our Lord had been saying these same sonship words every day, and all His days; and accordingly these same sonship words came naturally and fully and finally to His believing lips at the end of His days. For one thing, He had prayed, and that without ceasing, for thirty years, for the conversion of His unbelieving brothers and sisters at home in Nazareth. And hitherto He had prayed, as it seemed, in vain. And worse, it seemed, than in vain. For, year after year, they all seemed to go farther away from their true salvation than ever before. And yet, in all that, Christ may only have been made more and more like to you and to me. For years, year after year, some of you may have been praying and waiting for the true conversion of some one or more dear to you; and like your Lord, you may have to die and to leave them as they were, only worse. And *that* may well be *the* cross of all your crosses on your death-bed.

My brethren, travellers in the Holy Land tell us that the Jordan is sometimes very mysterious, very dark, very deep, very crooked, and sometimes very angry, and without a bridge to cross it or a ford to wade it. It was so to your Lord, and it is enough for this life that the disciple be as his Lord was. My brethren, if the Son of God and the Prince of believers and your great High Priest had to say, as He looked around on His unconverted family circle, "Thy will be done," it is enough for you to be able to say the same thing. But what you are never to know here of the dark mystery of your unanswered prayer, you will certainly know hereafter: even as *He now knows*.

And then, Paul's old age and the nearness of his Jordan have taught many old men, and especially many old ministers, this lesson. "I am now ready to be offered, and the time of my departure is at hand. Do thy diligence therefore to come to me shortly. And bring with thee the cloak I left at Troas, and the books, and especially the parchments." And so it is with some of the successors of the book-loving apostle. You will go into the old-age chamber of some of your ministers and you will find near their chair, and near their bed, such old-age books and such Jordan-bank books as these: John's Revelation open at the twenty-first and twenty-second chapters; and Dante's *Paradise;* and Bunyan's *Pilgrim's Progress;* and Baxter's *Saints' Rest;* and Howe's *Blessedness of the Righteous;* and Rutherford's *Letters;* and Newman's *Dream of Gerontius;* and the *Olney* and the *Wesley Hymns*. Many years ago, I went into the death-chamber of an elder of this congregation and he laid his hand on the *Westminster Confession of Faith* lying open at the great chapter on Justification; and he said to me, "Sir, I am dying in the strength of that peace-seeking chapter." Do thy diligence to bring the right books, as soon as possible, wrote Paul to Timothy, his son in the Gospel.

And all men who are of a philosophic turn of mind will take *their* lesson from Bishop Butler's death-bed. "Him that cometh unto Me," said the Saviour, "I will in no wise cast out."

> I've read a thousand times that Scripture o'er,
> Nor felt its truth till now I near the tomb:
> It is enough! O Saviour Christ, I come.

"It was Bishop Butler who made me a Christian," said Dr. Chalmers to his students, generously confessing his indebtedness to the great philosopher. Let us all, like Dr. Chalmers, take the same philosopher for our everyday example, this day and every day, till we take him for our example on the last day of our earthly pilgrimage, and for our Jordan-side example, and say with him: "O Lamb of God, I come."

> Just as I am, without one plea
> But that Thy blood was shed for me,
> And that Thou bidd'st me come to Thee,
> O Lamb of God, I come.
>
> Just as I am, and waiting not
> To rid my soul of one dark blot,
> To Thee, whose blood can cleanse each spot,
> O Lamb of God, I come.
>
> Just as I am, though tossed about
> With many a conflict, many a doubt,
> Fightings and fears within, without,
> O Lamb of God, I come.
>
> Just as I am, of that free love
> The breadth, length, depth, and height to prove,
> Here for a season, then above,
> O Lamb of God, I come. Amen.

"And then shall the King say unto them on His right hand: Come, ye blessed of My Father, inherit the Kingdom prepared for you from the foundation of the world."

And to all who so come to Him, and who keep so coming, He will surely say: "When thou passest through the waters, I will be with thee, and through the rivers, they shall not overflow thee"; "till the redeemed of the Lord shall return, and shall come to Zion with songs and with everlasting joy upon their heads: they shall obtain joy and gladness, and sorrow and sighing shall flee away."

22

The Hebrew Child's Question at the Passover Supper

It shall come to pass, when your children shall say unto you, What mean ye by this service? that ye shall say, It is the sacrifice of the Lord's passover. (Exod. 12:26-27).

Had you been a sojourner in any Hebrew house, on any Passover night in Old Testament times, you would have seen and heard all this. You would have seen the head of the house killing a lamb, and sprinkling its blood on the doorpost of the house. The flesh of the lamb was then roasted, and was eaten along with unleavened bread and bitter herbs. And all the assembled family ate their Passover supper standing on their feet, with their loins girt and with their staff in their hand; and all that in haste, as if they were all ready for a midnight escape.

And always, at this point of the ordinance, the eldest son of the house came forward and said to his father: "What mean ye by this service?" And the head of the house always gave the same prescribed reply: "This is the sacrifice of the Lord's Passover, who *passed over* the houses of our fathers in Egypt, when He smote the Egyptians, and delivered His covenanted people." And once every year, all down the generations, the same scene was enacted, till we see, now the child David, and now the child Solomon, and now the child Isaiah, and now the child Daniel, and now the child Jesus of Nazareth, and now the child Saul of Tarsus—all asking the same question, and all receiving the same answer.

Now, it cannot fail to be both interesting and instructive to us this morning, if we follow the example of the Hebrew households, and bring forward, now a young communicant, and now a foreign student, to ask what is our Lord's meaning, and what is our meaning in this and in that part of our Communion service. For there will be young communicants here this morning, whose hunger for yet fuller teaching has only been whetted by what they have been taught at home and in the Communion class. Like the Child Jesus, who, just because He had asked the question of the text, and had received the answer of the text, every Passover night in Nazareth, was only all the more found in the Temple at His first Passover in Jerusalem, sitting in the midst of the doctors, both hearing them and asking them questions. Or again, there will be some divinity student here, from Africa or from India, or from China or from Japan, who is seeing for the first time the Lord's Supper dispensed in all its fullness, and in all its orderliness, and who, student-like, is not willing to let any part of the service pass till he has fully and clearly understood the whole Communion ordinance as it is observed in the long evangelised and long covenanted land of Scotland.

Now, that being so, I can imagine a young communicant coming forward at the opening of the service this morning and saying that he thinks he understands why this ordinance is called sometimes "The New Testament Passover," and sometimes "The Lord's Supper," and sometimes "The Communion." But he was reading an English Church Catechism the other evening, when he came on another name that he is not sure he fully understands. And that somewhat difficult Episcopal name is the "Eucharist." Well, that is a quite fit and proper question to ask. And this is my answer to that question. *Eucharist* is an untranslated Greek word, which means *the giving of thanks*. And you will remember how the Gospels tell us again and again that our Lord began the Paschal Supper that night by giving thanks to His Father in heaven. We read that fact again and again. But it is not so easily understood just why He gave thanks for the bread and for the wine, and for all that the broken bread and poured out wine symbolised that New Testament Passover night. I can quite easily understand Peter and James and John giving great thanks for the Lord's Table, because they were great sinners. But that was just what their Master was not. "He knew no sin"; and therefore He did not need the redemption from sin that was set forth by that broken bread and that poured out wine. For what then did He give thanks? For what, communicants, but for this, that it is far more blessed to give redemption than it is to receive it; and it was for that supreme blessedness of His, that night, that He gave His Father such heartfelt thanks, in these true and beautiful Communion lines of his:

> And could'st Thou, Lord, Thy thanks express
> In prospect of Thy deep distress?
> And at the Table, spread to show
> Thy symbols of Thy coming woe,
>
> And could'st Thou bless Thy God on high,
> That He had sent Thee thus to die,
> And for our sins to give Thee up
> To drink wrath's overwhelming cup?
>
> O! what a love must Thine have been!
> To *praise* in view of such a scene!
> When broken bread, and poured out wine,
> Portrayed those bitter woes of Thine.

Yes, I think my dear old friend has here given the true reply to your question about the Eucharist—that is to say, about our Saviour's giving of thanks at the table that night.

Again, you will all have observed that the first thing the officiating minister does at the head of the Table is to read what he calls the "warrant" for what he and the elders and the communicants are about to do. Now, what is a "warrant"? What is it but a permission, a sanction, a legalisation of something that is about to be done? But we take our place at the Lord's Table today on far stronger grounds than any mere warrant. For we came to His Table at our Lord's express desire and earnest wish; nay, we come at His express command. "Do this," He says, "in remembrance of Me." "Take, eat," He says, handing round the bread; "this is My body broken for you; this do in remembrance of Me." And, "This cup is the New Testament in My blood; therefore, this also do ye in remembrance of Me." "For," adds the apostle, "as often as ye eat this bread and drink this cup, ye do show forth the Lord's death till He come." So that, you see, we will neglect the Lord's Table at our peril; yes, at our peril, as we shall answer to Him, at His coming, for having boldly disobeyed His dying command, and for openly despising and trampling upon His body and His blood.

But then, on the other hand, there is what is called "fencing the Table." Now you all know at once what a fence is, for what purpose a shepherd runs a fence round his sheepfold. Well, all men, the very worst, are welcome, and at all times are welcome to the Saviour. There are no fences run around the Cross. But in the nature of things, all men are not welcome, as yet, to the Lord's Table. Why—the very apostle of free grace spends the half of his First Epistle to the sanctified in Corinth in running a strong and a sharp fence round the Lord's Table in that so corrupt city. And then, not apostles and pastors only are on occasion to fence the Lord's Table; but there are times and circumstances when intending communicants themselves are rigidly to fence themselves away from the Table. For, "it is required of them that would worthily partake of the Lord's Supper, that they examine themselves of their knowledge to discern the Lord's body, of their faith to feed upon Him, of their repentance, love, and new obedience: lest, coming unworthily, they eat and drink judgment to themselves." But then truly and properly speaking, no man is, or ever will be, worthy to partake of the Table of the Lord. But worthiness is one thing, when a communicant is looked at as he is in himself; and it is quite another thing when he is looked at as in Christ, and as invited and indeed commanded by Christ to come to His Table.

> I am not worthy; cold and bare
> The lodging of my soul;
> How canst thou deign to enter there?
> Lord, speak, and make me whole.
>
> O come, in this sweet morning hour
> Feed me with food divine;
> And fill with all Thy love and power
> This worthless heart of mine.

At this stage of our service, a divinity student, say from India, comes forward and says that, though he had often heard the Scottish missionaries speak of the *Shorter Catechism* with profound reverence, he had never had the least idea of the intellectual power and the spiritual depth of that scriptural document till he came to the New College and commenced to study divinity seriously and with all his might. And just last night when he was working his way through the sacramental chapters of the Catechism to prepare himself for this morning, he came on the passage that promised him "spiritual nourishment"—spiritual nourishment and growth in grace—at the table today. And he would like to learn more of what the Catechism means by "spiritual nourishment and growth in grace." Well, the answer is this: The communicant's body is not nourished at the Lord's Table, it is his soul. It is his spirit that is nourished here. "Let every man eat his own supper at home, for his bodily nourishment," says the Apostle. But he who would have his soul and spirit nourished to more and more spiritual and eternal life, let him come, by faith, to the Lord's Table. As Robert Bruce (that stately Presbyterian divine, as David Masson calls him) said in his Fourth Sermon on the Sacraments, delivered in the High Kirk of Edinburgh in the year 1590: "The flesh of Christ is not like any other eaten flesh. The flesh of Christ is such that it is really not my bodily but my spiritual nourishment. The flesh of Christ symbolised by the broken bread serves me to my spiritual life; and for this reason it is called my spiritual food. It is called spiritual in respect of the end and design for which I partake of it; because when I, by faith aright partake of it, I am thereby nourished not to a bodily life but to a spiritual and a heavenly life." Let every true student of the Sacraments read Robert Bruce in his so racy Scotch; and along with Bruce, Jonathan Edwards on the *Religious Affections*. Two masterly men to be read and read again by all true students of these divine matters. For my part, I read them both every pre-communion week.

Another thing that will have arrested the young communicants last week, as they read the history of the Lord's Supper as it was instituted that Passover night, was this: "A new commandment," said Christ to His disciples, "I give unto you at My Table: and that is that ever after this night you shall love one another, as I have loved you." A *new commandment*, He said, and with a great emphasis. And yet all the time that was an old commandment. That was a commandment as old as when man was first made in the image of the God of love. But all old things were made new that great new-creation night in the upper room. And that new commandment of brotherly love must have come home with new and poignant power even to the dullest mind and the hardest heart at that New Testament Table. For it was only yesterday that they had all scandalised their Master by the way they had "disputed" as they came up to Jerusalem to the Passover—disputed with a great heat as to who would be greatest in the coming Kingdom. And it was in His great shame and pain at the envious and angry quarrel that their Master poured water into a basin, and took a towel and washed their feet; as also, put into the hands of every one of them, Judas Iscariot and all, the broken bread and the poured out wine of His body and His blood. "As I have loved you, that ye go and love and serve one another," He said: "rejoicing in one another's greatness in My Kingdom, more than in your own greatness therein." Yes, a new commandment, because issued on such a new ground that Lord's Supper night.

During the dispensation of the Lord's Supper that night, six of the twelve disciples came forward and put Passover questions to their Master. Judas and Peter and John, and Thomas and Philip and Judas, not Iscariot, all put Passover questions to Him; and we have the answers that they all got. But there was one thing that our Lord said and did that night, concerning which no one seems to have felt any difficulty, or started any inquiry. "Verily," He said, "I will drink no more of the fruit of the vine, till I drink it new with you in the Kingdom of God." What did He mean? What exactly did He mean them and us to understand by that mysterious saying of His? This, I think: all the old things of this world are to be made new in the Kingdom of God, and all our old wines among them. When He who sits upon the throne has made all things new, there will be new heavens and a new earth. There will be a new Jerusalem, and in the new Jerusalem a new upper room. There will be new vineyards, and new vines in that Holy Land—our Heavenly Father all the time abiding the Husbandman.

And then will be fulfilled the great promise made of old to the evangelical prophet: "Now will I sing to my well-beloved a song of my beloved touching his vineyard. My well-beloved hath a vineyard in a very fruitful hill. And I the Lord do keep it: I will water it every moment: and lest any hurt it, I will keep it night and day." And then, when all the trees of Paradise restored shall say to that vine: "Come thou and reign over us," then shall that heavenly vine answer them and say: "How shall I leave my wine, which cheereth and maketh glad the heart of God and man, and go to be promoted over the other trees? No, I will not." And then, concerning that new wine, it will never be said: "Look not on it when it is red: when it giveth his colour in the cup," for that heavenly wine will not bite like a serpent, and sting like an adder. But instead of that bitter proverb this sweet nuptial song shall be sung by the Bridegroom over the Bride: "I have drunk my wine with my milk. Eat, O friends; drink, yea, drink abundantly, O Beloved, of the running-over wine-cup of my everlasting love." Yes, communicants! *So* shall it be said to you all; and *so* shall it be done to you all, at the Marriage Supper of the Lamb.

Also from Kingsley Press:

AN ORDERED LIFE
AN AUTOBIOGRAPHY BY G. H. LANG

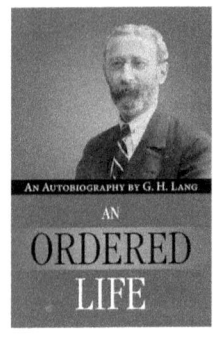

G. H. Lang was a remarkable Bible teacher, preacher and writer of a past generation who should not be forgotten by today's Christians. He inherited the spiritual "mantle" of such giants in the faith as George Müller, Anthony Norris Groves and other notable saints among the early Brethren movement. He traveled all over the world with no fixed means of support other than prayer and faith and no church or other organization to depend on. Like Mr. Müller before him, he told his needs to no one but God. Many times his faith was tried to the limit, as funds for the next part of his journey arrived only at the last minute and from unexpected sources.

This autobiography traces in precise detail the dealings of God with his soul, from the day of his conversion at the tender age of seven, through the twilight years when bodily infirmity restricted most of his former activities. You will be amazed, as you read these pages, to see how quickly and continually a soul can grow in grace and in the knowledge of spiritual things if they will wholly follow the Lord.

Horace Bushnell once wrote that every man's life is a plan of God, and that it's our duty as human beings to find and follow that plan. As Mr. Lang looks back over his long and varied life in the pages of this book, he frequently points out the many times God prepared him in the present for some future work or role. Spiritual life applications abound throughout the book, making it not just a life story but a spiritual training manual of sorts. Preachers will find sermon starters and illustrations in every chapter. Readers of all kinds will benefit from this close-up view of the dealings of God with the soul of one who made it his life's business to follow the Lamb wherever He should lead.

Buy online at our website: **www.KingsleyPress.com**
Also available as an eBook for Kindle, Nook and iBooks.

The Revival We Need

by Oswald J. Smith

When Oswald J. Smith wrote this book almost a hundred years ago he felt the most pressing need of the worldwide church was true revival—the kind birthed in desperate prayer and accompanied by deep conviction for sin, godly sorrow, and deep repentance, resulting in a living, victorious faith. If he were alive today he would surely conclude that the need has only become more acute with the passing years.

The author relates how there came a time in his own ministry when he became painfully aware that his efforts were not producing spiritual results. His intense study of the New Testament and past revivals only deepened this conviction. The Word of God, which had proved to be a hammer, a fire and a sword in the hands of apostles and revivalists of bygone days, was powerless in his hands. But as he prayed and sought God in dead earnest for the outpouring of the Holy Spirit, things began to change. Souls came under conviction, repented of their sins, and were lastingly changed.

The earlier chapters of the book contain Smith's heart-stirring messages on the need for authentic revival: how to prepare the way for the Spirit's moving, the tell-tale signs that the work is genuine, and the obstacles that can block up the channels of blessing. These chapters are laced with powerful quotations from revivalists and soul-winners of former times, such as David Brainerd, William Bramwell, John Wesley, Charles Finney, Evan Roberts and many others. The latter chapters detail Smith's own quest for the enduement of power, his soul-travail, and the spiritual fruit that followed.

In his foreword to this book, Jonathan Goforth writes, "Mr. Smith's book, *The Revival We Need*, for its size is the most powerful plea for revival I have ever read. He has truly been led by the Spirit of God in preparing it. To his emphasis for the need of a Holy Spirit revival I can give the heartiest amen. What I saw of revival in Korea and in China is in fullest accord with the revival called for in this book."

Buy online at our website: **www.KingsleyPress.com**
Also available as an eBook for Kindle, Nook and iBooks.

Lord, Teach Us to Pray
By Alexander Whyte

D r. Alexander Whyte (1836-1921) was widely acknowledged to be the greatest Scottish preacher of his day. He was a mighty pulpit orator who thundered against sin, awakening the consciences of his hearers, and then gently leading them to the Savior. He was also a great teacher, who would teach a class of around 500 young men after Sunday night service, instructing them in the way of the Lord more perfectly.

In the later part of Dr. Whyte's ministry, one of his pet topics was prayer. Luke 11:1 was a favorite text and was often used in conjunction with another text as the basis for his sermons on this subject. The sermons printed here represent only a few of the many delivered. But each one is deeply instructive, powerful and convicting.

Nobody else could have preached these sermons; after much reading and re-reading of them that remains the most vivid impression. There can be few more strongly personal documents in the whole literature of the pulpit. . . . When all is said, there is something here that defies analysis—something titanic, something colossal, which makes ordinary preaching seem to lie a long way below such heights as gave the vision in these words, such forces as shaped their appeal. We are driven back on the mystery of a great soul, dealt with in God's secret ways and given more than the ordinary measure of endowment and grace. His hearers have often wondered at his sustained intensity; as Dr. Joseph Parker once wrote of him: "many would have announced the chaining of Satan for a thousand years with less expenditure of vital force" than Dr. Whyte gave to the mere announcing of a hymn. —*From the Preface*

Buy online at our website: **www.KingsleyPress.com**
Also available as an eBook for Kindle, Nook and iBooks.

The Way of the Cross
by J. Gregory Mantle

"DYING to self is the *one only way* to life in God," writes Dr. Mantle in this classic work on the cross. "The end of self is the one condition of the promised blessing, and he that is not willing to die to things sinful, *yea, and to things lawful,* if they come between the spirit and God, cannot enter that world of light and joy and peace, provided on this side of heaven's gates, where thoughts and wishes, words and works, delivered from the perverting power of self—revolve round Jesus Christ, as the planets revolve around the central sun....

"It is a law of dynamics that two objects cannot occupy the same space at the same time, and if we are ignorant of the crucifixion of the self-life as an experimental experience, we cannot be filled with the Holy Spirit. 'If thy heart,' says Arndt in his *True Christianity*, 'be full of the world, there will be no room for the Spirit of God to enter; for where the one is the other cannot be.' If, on the contrary, we have endorsed our Saviour's work as the destroyer of the works of the devil, and have claimed to the full the benefits of His death and risen life, what hinders the complete and abiding possession of our being by the Holy Spirit but our unbelief?"

Rev. J. Gregory Mantle (1853 - 1925) *had a wide and varied ministry in Great Britain, America, and around the world. For many years he was the well-loved Superintendent of the flourishing Central Hall in Deptford, England, as well as a popular speaker at Keswick and other large conventions for the deepening of spiritual life. He spent the last twelve years of his life in America, where he was associated with Dr. A. B. Simpson and the Christian and Missionary Alliance. He traveled extensively, holding missions and conventions all over the States. He was an avid supporter of foreign missions throughout his entire career. He also edited a missionary paper, and wrote several books.*

GIPSY SMITH
HIS LIFE AND WORK

This autobiography of Gipsy Smith (1860-1947) tells the fascinating story of how God's amazing grace reached down into the life of a poor, uneducated gipsy boy and sent him singing and preaching all over Britain and America until he became a household name in many parts and influenced the lives of millions for Christ. He was born and raised in a gipsy tent to parents who made a living selling baskets, tinware and clothes pegs. His father was in and out of jail for various offences, but was gloriously converted during an evangelistic meeting. His mother died when he was only five years old.

Converted at the age of sixteen, Gipsy taught himself to read and write and began to practice preaching. His beautiful singing voice earned him the nickname "the singing gipsy boy," as he sang hymns to the people he met. At age seventeen he became an evangelist with the Christian Mission (which became the Salvation Army) and began to attract large crowds. Leaving the Salvation Army in 1882, he became an itinerant evangelist working with a variety of organizations. It is said that he never had a meeting without conversions. He was a born orator. One of the Boston papers described him as "the greatest of his kind on earth, a spiritual phenomenon, an intellectual prodigy and a musical and oratorical paragon."

His autobiography is full of anedotes and stories from his preaching experiences in many different places. It's a book you won't want to put down until you're finished!

Buy online at our website: **www.KingsleyPress.com**
Also available as an eBook for Kindle, Nook and iBooks.

THE AWAKENING
By Marie Monsen

REVIVAL! It was a long time coming. For twenty long years Marie Monsen prayed for revival in China. She had heard reports of how God's Spirit was being poured out in abundance in other countries, particularly in nearby Korea; so she began praying for funds to be able to travel there in order to bring back some of the glowing coals to her own mission field. But that was not God's way. The still, small voice of God seemed to whisper, "What is happening in Korea can happen in China if you will pay the price in prayer." Marie Monsen took up the challenge and gave her solemn promise: "Then I will pray until I receive."

The Awakening is Miss Monsen's own vivid account of the revival that came in answer to prayer. Leslie Lyall calls her the "pioneer" of the revival movement—the handmaiden upon whom the Spirit was first poured out. He writes: "Her surgical skill in exposing the sins hidden within the Church and lurking behind the smiling exterior of many a trusted Christian—even many a trusted Christian leader—and her quiet insistence on a clear-cut experience of the new birth set the pattern for others to follow."

The emphasis in these pages is on the place given to prayer both before and during the revival, as well as on the necessity of self-emptying, confession, and repentance in order to make way for the infilling of the Spirit.

One of the best ways to stir ourselves up to pray for revival in our own generation is to read the accounts of past awakenings, such as those found in the pages of this book. Surely God is looking for those in every generation who will solemnly take up the challenge and say, with Marie Monsen, "I will pray until I receive."

Buy online at our website: **www.KingsleyPress.com**
Also available as an eBook for Kindle, Nook and iBooks.

FIRSTFRUITS AND HARVEST
By G. H. Lang

Few writers have approached the subject of Biblical prophecy with more diligence and precise thinking than G. H. Lang. His purpose in studying and writing on the end-times and related themes was not to be controversial or sensational, but rather to encourage watchfulness and readiness. The serious reader will find much to challenge both mind and heart in these pages as the writer uses the prophetic Scriptures to give a strong call to holy and careful living.

The secret of G. H. Lang's power and persuasiveness as a writer must surely be attributed to his lifelong dedication to searching the Scriptures, not for the sake of aquiring more knowledge, but in order that he might know God more intimately and follow Him more closely. His great passion was that God's children everywhere would press beyond the shallow and superficial and into a deep understanding of the ways and workings of God. In this respect he was the true successor to such spiritual giants as George Müller, Hudson Taylor, Robert Cleaver Chapman and Anthony Norris Groves.

One of Mr. Lang's contemporaries, Douglas W. Brealey, wrote of him: "I think I may truthfully say that he was the most apostolic man I have ever met; perhaps for that very reason he was a very controversial figure; a correspondent suggested to me that he was the most controversial figure in Brethren circles since J. N. Darby; yet it would be true to say that he himself was not a controversialist. A very close student of the Word, and an independent thinker, he was not prepared to take traditional interpretations unless he were personally convinced that they were right.... To be in his presence was to realize that one was in the presence of a true saint of God whose holy life gave weight and authority to all he taught."

Buy online at our website: www.KingsleyPress.com
Also available as an eBook for Kindle, Nook and iBooks.

The Churches of God
by G. H. Lang

If you've ever wondered what the churches of the New Testament looked like—how they functioned, how they were governed, how they conducted their evangelistic and missionary enterprises, what ordinances they observed, what their liturgy consisted of, how decisions were made, how discipline was administered; if you've ever wondered how far modern churches have drifted from the New Testament pattern; if you've ever wondered what it would take for your church, and others like it, to return to the New Testament model, or if such a thing is even possible or desirable—then this book is for you!

G. H. Lang's ability to elucidate Biblical truth was never more evident than in this small treatise on the constitution, government, discipline and ministry of the church of God. His gifts as a diligent Bible student, expositor, and precise thinker, together with his many years of experience as an itinerant Bible teacher in many different countries and cultural settings, all combine to make this a go-to reference on many issues relating to the local church.

About the Author

G. H. Lang (1874-1958) was a gifted Bible teacher and prolific author who in his early life was associated with the "exclusive" branch of the Plymouth Brethren but later affiliated himself with the Open Brethren. He traveled widely as an itinerant Bible teacher, depending solely on God for his support. Although Mr. Lang himself was a prolific author, it was his belief that "no man should write a book until he is 40. He needs to prove his theories in practice before publishing." In his own case, all but nine of his many books were written after he was 50. Kingsley Press has recently re-published Lang's amazing autobiography, *An Ordered Life*. More information can be found on our web site: www.KingsleyPress.com.

A Present Help
By Marie Monsen

Does your faith in the God of the impossible need reviving? Do you think that stories of walls of fire and hosts of guardian angels protecting God's children are only for Bible times? Then you should read the amazing accounts in this book of how God and His unseen armies protected and guided Marie Monsen, a Norwegian missionary to China, as she traveled through bandit-ridden territory spreading the Gospel of Jesus Christ and standing on the promises of God. You will be amazed as she tells of an invading army of looters who ravaged a whole city, yet were not allowed to come near her mission compound because of angels standing sentry over it. Your heart will thrill as she tells of being held captive on a ship for twenty-three days by pirates whom God did not allow to harm her, but instead were compelled to listen to her message of a loving Savior who died for their sin. As you read the many stories in this small volume your faith will be strengthened by the realization that our God is a living God who can still bring protection and peace in the midst of the storms of distress, confusion and terror—a very present help in trouble.

Buy online at our website: **www.KingsleyPress.com**
Also available as an eBook for Kindle, Nook and iBooks.

ANTHONY NORRIS GROVES
SAINT AND PIONEER
by G. H. Lang

Although his name is little known in Christian cirlces today, Anthony Norris Groves (1795-1853) was, according to the writer of this book, one of the most influential men of the nineteenth century. He was what might be termed a spiritual pioneer, forging a path through unfamiliar territory in order that others might follow. One of those who followed him was George Müller, known to the world as one who in his lifetime cared for over ten thousand orphans without any appeal for human aid, instead trusting God alone to provide for the daily needs of this large enterprise.

In 1825 Groves wrote a booklet called *Christian Devotedness* in which he encouraged fellow believers and especially Christian workers to take literally Jesus' command not to lay up treasures on earth, but rather to give away their savings and possessions toward the spread of the gospel and to embark on a life of faith in God alone for the necessaries of life. Groves himself took this step of faith: he gave away his fortune, left his lucrative dental practice in England, and went to Baghdad to establish the first Protestant mission to Arabic-speaking Muslims. His going was not in connection with any church denomination or missionary society, as he sought to rely on God alone for needed finances. He later went to India also.

His approach to missions was to simplify the task of churches and missions by returning to the methods of Christ and His apostles, and to help indigenous converts form their own churches without dependence on foreign support. His ideas were considered radical at the time but later became widely accepted in evangelical circles.

Groves was a leading figure in the early days of what Robert Govett would later call the mightiest movement of the Spirit of God since Pentecost—a movement that became known simply as the Brethren. In this book G. H. Lang combines a study of the life and influence of Anthony Norris Groves with a survey of the original principles and practices of the Brethren movement.

MEMOIRS OF DAVID STONER

Edited by
William Dawson & John Hannah

The name of David Stoner (1794-1826) deserves to be ranked alongside those of Robert Murray McCheyne, David Brainerd and Henry Martyn. Like them, he died at a relatively young age; and like them, his life was marked by a profound hunger and thirst for God and intense passion for souls. Stoner was saved at twelve years of age and from that point until his untimely death twenty years later his soul was continually on full stretch for God.

This book tells the story of his short but amazing life: his godly upgringing, his radical conversion, his call to preach, his amazing success as a Wesleyan Methodist preacher, his patience in tribulation and sickness, and his glorious departure to be with Christ forever. Many pages are devoted to extracts from his personal diary which give an amazing glimpse into the heart of one whose desires were all aflame for more of God.

Oswald J. Smith, in his soul-stirring book, *The Revival We Need*, wrote the following: "Have been reading the diary of David Stoner. How I thank God for it! He is another Brainerd. Have been much helped, but how ashamed and humble I feel as I read it! Oh, how he thirsted and searched after God! How he agonized and travailed! And he died at 32."

You, too can be much helped in your spiritual life as you study the life of this youthful saint of a past generation.

"Be instant and constant in prayer. Study, books, eloquence, fine sermons are all nothing without prayer. Prayer brings the Spirit, the life, the power." —*David Stoner*

Buy online at our website: **www.KingsleyPress.com**
Also available as an eBook for Kindle, Nook and iBooks.

www.ingramcontent.com/pod-product-compliance
Lightning Source LLC
Chambersburg PA
CBHW071457040426
42444CB00008B/1376